FIELD GUIDE
TO
HAUNTED HIGHWAYS & BRIDGES
BY
DALE KACZMAREK

A Ghost Research Society Press Publication

This Book Is Published By
Ghost Research Society Press
P.O. Box 205
Oak Lawn, Illinois, 60454
(708) 425-5163
http://www.ghostresearch.org/press.html

First Printing – May 2012
ISBN: 978-0-9797115-5-8

Printed in the United States of America

This book is dedicated to three very great paranormal researchers and investigators whom have recently gone over to the other side themselves; Ed Warren, the great Hans Holzer and Dr. William Roll. You will all be missed!

HAUNTED FIELD GUIDE SERIES

Welcome to the ninth book in the Haunted Field Guide Series that was created by Jim Graczyk. Ghost Research Society Press is dedicated to providing the readers with these "field guides" to not only haunted places, but to ghost research as well. In the books to come, we will take you beyond the cities and provide detailed listings and directions to haunted places all over the Midwest and America. The series plans to devote books to various types of ghost research, investigations, and much more.

We hope you enjoy this series and that you will journey with us in the future as we take you past the limits of hauntings in America and beyond the farthest reaches of your imagination!

Happy Hauntings!

I would like to thank the following people, websites or groups for submitting material, photographs or allowing me to use material from their investigations in the writing of this book; Nicole Strickland, Dave Juliano of the Shadowlands Website (www.theshadowlands.net), Faith Serafin of the Alabama Ghost Hunters (www.alabamaghosthunters.com), Dennis William Hauck, Preston Dennett, Greg Bishop, Joe Oesterle, Mike Marinacci, George Houde from Copley Press, Chris Dedman, Route 66 Paranormal Alliance, Haunted Road (www.freewebs.com/hauntedroad), Rick Crawford, Bruce Cline of Little Egypt Ghost Society, Wikipedia, Bridgehunter.com, Vincent Gaddis's book *Mysterious Fire and Lights* and my many friends on Facebook that help steer me in the right direction with additional leads, websites, people to interview or obscure stories not commonly known.

Plus all those hard-working paranormal groups whose diligence and perseverance in never-ending research and investigation into these and many more sites help make this book possible. To each and every one of you and for those I inadvertently overlooked a big thank you!

Introduction

One night while security guards were watching satellite footage they noticed a group of children playing under Pearoyd Bridge. Even stranger than seeing a group of children out at night playing was that the clothes that they were wearing looked as those you would have seen in the past. The children did not look like they were from modern times! This prompted the guards to investigate, so they made their way to the bridge. When they arrived they found nothing, not a trace that anyone let alone children had been there. The muddy ground was untouched by feet and no one was around. Also in the same area workmen who were staying in campervans while working on the road reported that they could hear children singing at night.

On another night the guards again saw the ghostly appearance on the bridge. When patrolling the area they saw a monk-like figure standing on the bridge. This spooky sighting prompted them to call the police who quickly dismissed their report as a joke and told them to find a priest. When the men got this reply they did just as the police said, and the priest called the police. The police now had to give in and go to the site to check this out. When they first arrived they could see nothing but a few minutes later the temperature apparently got very cold and just beside their window they saw a body, clearly lacking a head, arms and legs! When they tried to escape, their car would not start on the first attempt.

To this day the monk and children have been sighted; drivers have reported the monk suddenly appearing beside them in their cars. Theories as to why this road is haunted are linked to the many pit shafts that are found in the area. It is thought that when they were operational a number of children fell into them and perished. The monk is thought to be the ghost of a monk that was once part of Hunshelf Priory and had become disillusioned.

This report comes from Stocksbridge, Sheffield, England but is surely nothing new or unique. Reports of haunted highways, roads, interstates whether they are new or antiquated can be found throughout the world. Many times these reports stem from untimely deaths, murders, suicides, or simply urban legends. Bridges built along these roads sometimes suffer the same type of legends and stories that are handed down from generation to generation.

There are dozens of reports of so-called "Cry Baby Bridges" and all seem to have a commonality. An infant or child is either thrown from the bridge or fell from its mother's arms only to drown in the water beneath. People passing over the bridge, usually at night, can sometime hear the sounds of a baby crying but no real human is ever found. It is apparently just the residual sounds of the tragedy being replayed over and over again. I've had a chance to visit a number of Cry Baby Bridges and haunted highways while researching this book but, to date, have never heard a baby cry and every Cry Baby Bridge out there today believes that "it' is the original one.

A great number of the stories in this book are impossible to substantiate and may be nothing more than urban legend but the stories and surely some of the colorful names are fascinating. Many of the names like Devil's Bridge, Cry Baby Bridge, Deadman's Curve and so forth aren't the real names of these locations, making them extremely hard to locate unless you are a local resident and know the story yourself. Painstaking research has gone into each and every story in an effort to locate at least the location of the road or bridge, GPS coordinates or directions from the largest major city or highway so that the reader can eventually visit the site if they so desire. While you might not find a ghost, you surely will run into a number of people at these sights that claim to have had an encounter or can fill you in on more of the details of the legend.

I have purposely left out a lot of locations that I found on the internet, word of mouth or obscure listings that could not be verified or actual locations found. I believe listing them in the book would be a disservice to the readers if you could not find the location to visit.

As with all locations, it is advisable never to travel to these obscure rural locations at night by yourself. Bring friends with you because there's safety in numbers. Always try to secure permission if you believe the area might be on private property or at least view it from a distance if you can't acquire such permission. Good luck and happy hauntings!

Table of Contents

Kern County/Bakersfield
    Lerdo Hwy 46
Lathrop
    Mossdale Bridge 46
Montecito
    Ortega Road 47
Pasadena
    Suicide Bridge 47
Salinas
    Old Stage Road 48
San Diego
    Cabrillo Bridge 49
    Coronado Bridge 50
San Francisco
    California St. 50
    Golden Gate Bridge 51
San Juan Capistrano
    Los Rios St. 52
    Ortega Hwy 53
Santa Clara County
    Pacheco Pass 53
Stockton
    Eight Mile Road 54
West Hollywood
    Laurel Canyon Blvd. 54

Colorado

Aurora
    Third Bridge #2 55
Bennett
    Train Bridge over Kiowa
    Creek 55
Thornton
    Riverdale Road 56

Connecticut

Kensington
    Chamberlain Hwy 57
Torrington
    Oak Avenue 57

Delaware

Frederica
    Hwy 12W 58
Newark
    Cooches Bridge 58
    Salem Church Road 58

Florida

Daytona Beach
    Orange Ave. Bridge 59

Gainesville
    Williston Road 59
Jacksonville
    Ghost Light Road 60
Lady Lake
    Rolling Acres Road 61
Marianna
    Bellamy Bridge 61

Georgia

Bartow County
    Hardin Bridge Road 63
Clarkesville
    Cannon Bridge 64
Colquitt
    Whites Bridge Road 64
Columbus
    Cry Baby Bridge 65
Newman
    Cedar Creek Bridge 65
Valdosta
    Spook Bridge 66
White County (Cleveland)
    Stovall Mill Bridge 67

Hawaii

Honolulu
    Hwy 1 68
    Old Pali Road 68

Idaho

Caldwell
    River Road Bridge 69

Illinois

Algonquin
    Square Barn Road 70
Barrington
    Cuba Road 70
    Rainbow Road 71
Benton
    Cry Baby Bridge 72
Burr Ridge
    German Church Road 73
Byron
    Kennedy Hill Road 75
Cherry Valley
    Bloods Point Road 77
Chicago
    49th & Loomis 77

Death Alley 78
Marquette Road & Ashland Ave. 79
Sheridan Road 80
Suicide Bridge 81
Collinsville
Lebanon Road 82
Country Club Hills
I-57 & Flossmoor Road 83
Crab Orchard Lake
Rt. 13 84
East Dundee
Duncan Ave.
Elmhurst
Lake St. & Frontage Rd 88
Hickory Hills
95th & Kean 89
Werewolf Run 90
Justice
Archer Ave. 91
Kean Ave. 92
Why Not Drive-In 92
Lombard
St. Charles & Grace 93
Midlothian
Bachelor's Grove Road 94
Millstadt
Hernando's Bridge/Zingg Rd 95
Palatine
Palatine & Ela Roads 96
Palos Park
123rd & LaGrange Road 97
St. Charles
Munger Road 97
Steger
Axman's Bridge 98
Steger Road & Western Ave. 99
Watseka
Red Lantern Road 100

Indiana

Avon
White Lick Creek Bridge 101
Boonville
Elizaville Road 103
Bremen
Troll Bridge 103
Chesterton
Rt. 6 Bridge 104

Columbus
Haunted Bridge 105
Ft. Wayne
Bostick Bridge 106
Francisville
Moody Lane 107
Greencastle
Edna Collin's Bridge 108
Griffith
Reeder Road 109
Lowell
Indiana Bridge 110
173rd & Holttz Road 110
Michigan City
Devil's Bridge 111
Mulberry
Hamilton Road 112
Portage
Old Porter Road 112
Princeton
Bulldog Bridge 113
South Bend
Primose Road 113

Iowa

Boone
Kate Shelly High Bridge 115
Viola
Matt's Bridge 115

Kansas

Barnes
Coon Creek Bridge 117
Emporia
Bird Bridge 117
Valley Center/Wichita
Theorosa's Bridge 118

Kentucky

Corbin
Florence Road 120
Garrard County
Camp Nelson Bridge 120
Harrodsburg
Hank's Bridge 121
Lexington
Eyeball Bridge 121

New York

Angola
    Holland Road 165
Clinton Corners
    Fiddler's Bridge 166
Huntington
    Sweet Hollow Road 167
Montebello
    Old Spook Rock Road 168

North Carolina

Asheville
    Helen's Bridge 170
Brusnwick
    Mt. Misery Road 171
Jamestown
    Lydia's Bridge 172
Smithfield
    Mill Creek Bridge 173
Statesville
    Bostian Bridge 174

North Dakota

Leroy
    White Lady Road 176

Ohio

Amelia
    Dead Man's Curve 177
Ashland
    Rt. 42 tunnel 178
Batavia
    Lucy Run Road 178
Byron
    Trebein Road 179
Columbus
    Watkins Road Bridge 180
Dayton
    Bessie Little Bridge 180
Fremont
    Tindall Bridge 181
Gratis
    Brubaker Bridge 182
Lancaster
    Johnston Bridge 183
Mansfield
    Reformatory Road 184

Overton
    Leroy's Bridge 185
Oxford
    Buckley Road 186
Shunk
    Turkeyfoot Creek Bridge 186
Sugar Grove
    Hummell Bridge 187

Oklahoma

Oklahoma City
    Kitchen Lake Bridge 188
Quapaw
    Spook Light Road 189
Sand Springs
    Cimarron Turnpike 189

Oregon

Culver
    Old Hwy 97 191
Salem
    Crossian Creek Road 192

Pennsylvania

Altoona
    Beulah Road 193
Gettysburg
    Sach's Bridge 194
Girard
    Gudgeonville Bridge 195
Montandon
    Rishel Bridge 197
New Hope
    Van Sant Bridge 198
Wexford
    Blue Myst Road 198

South Carolina

Dillion
    I-95 Bingham's Light 200
Greenville
    Poinsett Bridge 201
Summerville
    Hwy 27 & Hwy 61 202

Tennessee

    Elizabethtown
        Smalling Bridge 203
    Sunbright
        Burnt Mill Bridge 204

Texas

    Anson
        Bridge 205
    Denton
        Goatman's Bridge 206

    Hutto
        Jake's Hill Bridge 208
    San Marcos
        Thompson Island Bridge 209
    Saratoga
        Bragg Road 210

Vermont

    Stowe
        Emily's Bridge 212

Virginia

    Belfast
        Rt. 19 213
    Clifton
        Bunnyman Bridge 214
    Suffolk
        Jackson Road 215

Washington

    Pasco
        US Hwy 395 217
    Purdy
        Purdy Bridge 217
    Seattle
        Suicide Bridge 218

Wisconsin

    Boltonville
        7 Bridge Road/Jay Rd 220
    McFarland
        Dyerson Road 221
    Stevens Point
        Red Bridge 222

ALABAMA

Alexander City 35010

Oakachoy Covered Bridge

Alexander City is a city in Tallapoosa County and it is locally known as Alex City. Alexander City was incorporated in 1872 as Youngstown, after its founder James Young. In 1873 the Savannah and Memphis Railroad came to the city. The city was later renamed in honor of the railroad's President Edward Porter-Alexander, hero of the Battle of Gettysburg for the Confederate States. On June 13, 1902 a huge fire almost completely destroyed the city.

The Oakachoy Covered Bridge was built by Melton Harris of homelands timber at a cost of $400.00 connecting Rockford in Coosa County and Dadeville in Tallapoosa County.

All that remains of the bridge today are the stone foundations and a wooden post on the east side of the creek which shows obvious charring.

Even though the bridge is gone, it is said the site is still haunted by a slave who was lynched and eventually hung inside the bridge. The bridge wasn't built until after 1916 well after the American Civil War so the slave connection is a bit dubious.

It is said that if you visit the bridge at exactly 12:05am and turn off your car lights, your doors will lock themselves and your car will start. Supposedly the slave was hung for fooling around with the landowner's wife.

Andalusia 36421

Prestwood Bridge

The Prestwood family is thought by many to have actually built the town of Andalusia. They arrived in Covington County from Coffee County in 1874. James Austin "Aus" Prestwood, a teenager whose father was killed during the Civil War was the first to begin building his dream that later became the town of Andalusia. In 1886, Aus purchased tracts of land given up by the Central Railroad and Banking Company of Georgia for back taxes. He brought railroad service to this part of the country and eventually donated land which was used for the building of the train depot and the Henderson family for the construction of the Henderson Building on the Court Square. He owned a cotton gin and the hotel which bears his name. He served as postmaster from 1883 to 1889 and one of his lasting achievements was the erection of the Prestwood Bridge across the Conecuh River.

How or why the bridge got a reputation for becoming haunted is not known but apparently locals believe if you stop on the bridge and turn off your headlights, something or someone will come and band loudly on your car even though nothing is visibly seen at the time. This idea of car headlights will come into play many times in stories throughout the book and I have seen similar stories associated with spooklights. The idea there is that you stop your car, flash your lights a number of times, depending on the story told, and the Spooklight will suddenly appear as if answering the blinking of your lights.

Attalla 35954

Attalla Wooden Bridge

The history of Attalla actually predates its incorporation as a town. LaFayette visited what later became the town of Attalla in 1825. The town adopted the name from a French writer, Courter B. Chateaubriand, who wrote a novel on "Atala, an Indian maiden." Attalla was incorporated on February 5, 1872, after being founded in 1870 on land donated for the site of the town by W.C. Hammond who was a plantation owner. However the town itself actually occupied the site of an Indian village and was the home of Captain John Brown, a famous Indian.

One of the very famous and often repeated urban legends has its home right on an old wooden bridge. According to legend, a school bus loaded with children overturned and fell off the bridge and into the lake, killing many onboard. Locals say that the ghosts of those unfortunate victims still roam the area of the bridge at night trying to prevent a similar accident from befalling you. If one stops their automobile front tires on the right side of the bridge at night and then shift the car into neutral, the ghosts of the children will actually push the car completely across the bridge so that the same accident isn't repeated again.

This story has been circulated around the country and some even add in an additional little bit extra for good measure. Before you approach the bridge, dust the bumper, trunk and entire back end of your automobile with baby powder and then stop the car on the bridge and place it in neutral. After the car is pushed to the other side, if you examine the back of the car, you will dozens of little handprints said to be that of the children's ghosts that just finished their good deed!

In most, if not all, of these stories, there was never such a tragic accident and the car moving over has a completely logically explanation. While it does appear that you are being pushed sometimes even uphill, it's really an optical illusion and the lay of the land is really sloping downward, so you are only truly coasting downhill and not being pushed at all. And the handprints? These were probably already there as there are oils on our hands that when powder is applied soaks through the powder and is absorbed, leaving behind handprints of real people that have touched the back of the car sometime in the past.

Bayview 35201

Bayview Bridge
GPS: 33.520279, -86.811508

Bayview is a community in Birmingham and is built around beautiful Bayview Lake. It is part of the Birmingham-Hoover-Cullman Combined Statistical Area. It was developed as a company town by the Tennessee Coal, Iron and Railroad Company.

Reports have seen a woman walking across the bridge in her wedding dress. According to legend, she ran away from her wedding and while crossing the bridge her car plummeted off the bridge into the waters below. Some even report what appears to be a white dress floating in the water near the bridge from time to time.

Birmingham 35261

Sicard Hollow Road
GPS: 33.450935, -86.717628

Supposedly this road was part of the original Alabama Interstate before being bypassed by the modern interstate. It is said that driving up and down the road at night in your car, occupants can feel a very strange energy given off by the road itself. A number of local groups have been out there and have taken unusual pictures of figures and sometimes orbs and streaks of light. Not much more is known currently about the past history of the site or any tragedies which might have contributed to the hauntings.

Camp Hill 36850

Loveladies Bridge

09/30/2007 12:16 AM

Photo courtesy of Alabama Ghost Hunters

There are a couple variations of this ghost story but both circulate around a woman who apparently died at the bridge. Some say she was a prostitute from nearby Reeltown of the Lovelady family. After becoming pregnant by a married man who later rejected her, deep in grief and melancholy, she jumped to her death from the bridge located on Lovelady and Prospect Road.

The other story is quite different and goes back over twenty years ago. Allegedly a woman and her infant died in a car accident on the bridge. Local legend relates that if you walk to the middle of the bridge at night and say, "Lovelady, Lovelady, I got your baby!" three times, she will appear on the opposite end of the bridge and slowly walk towards you to retrieve her child. That's a scary and creepy thought and I'm sure its one of those tests of manhood to go out there and try it.

Photo courtesy of Alabama Ghost Hunters

One night in particular the ghost research team, Alabama Ghost Hunters, brought an arsenal of equipment along with fresh batteries and chargers to keep their gear operational. As they gathered their gear and headed for the bridge co-founder, Cassie Clark and Reeltown associate and resident Jody Gann began to notice numerous technical problems with the equipment. Not just one but all three digital cameras began to malfunction and shut off even after they replaced the batteries. Then one of their hand-held video cameras failed to work on the bridge but once off the bridge on either side, the camera began to function properly again. Digital recorders would also either shut down completely or record only static; almost as if someone had thrown water into the microphone or speaker. Temperature readings taken that evening measured as much as 30 degree temperature drops. On warm summer nights, in 70 degree heat, the bridge would get very cold. Cold enough where you can actually see your breath!

"We've done a lot of research on the legends and have not been able to find anything to validate them. However, we do believe that 'something' is there on that bridge," founder Faith Serafin of Alabama Ghost Hunters recently wrote to tell me. "It may not be a screaming woman looking for her infant child but the strange static that floats in the air there and numerous difficulties we have with our technical devices tells me that whatever is there may not want to be seen or heard. It's definitely not a place for amateur ghost hunters since Lovelady Bridge is located on a busy road and with no lights surrounding the location, its difficult to see anything at all," Serafin says.

(Credit: Faith Serafin, Alabama Ghost Hunters)

Clanton 35045

Bridge in Refuge

Alfred Baker founded the town of Clanton in 1868 when Chilton County was formed. The town was named in honor of General James H. Clanton, a general in the CSA and was officially incorporated on April 23, 1873. During the Second World War a small German POW camp was located in Clanton. GPS: 32.839810, -86.628188

Located along Refuge Road (CR 32) is a small, one-lane bridge. Visitors who travel there at night complain of hearing strange sounds and seeing balls of lights. When the brave get out of their car for closer examination, many feel a menacing presence come right up close to them. Some have been chased by strange unearthly fogs while others report their automobiles will begin to rock from side to side. Locals believe that there is an area nearby where nothing seems to be able to grow and it appears to be completely dead. A great evil is often experienced out here.

Cry Baby Bridge

There is even some confusion between this Cry Baby Bridge and the Bridge in Refuge and some locals believe it may be the same bridge due to its description as being very old, wooden and rickety. This is the first of many Cry Baby Bridge we will examine and the story here has another twist. Even though the story doesn't make much sense, here it is.

It is told that a long time ago when a war was waging (Vietnam, WWII??) and during a foggy night, a woman had given birth to a child.

For some unknown reason some men were chasing her in an attempt to kill the child, so she threw her baby into the creek where it drowned. People visiting the site today report hearing the sound of a baby crying but none is ever found. In order to appease the child, visitors leave unwrapped candy bars on the bridge but before they leave, they turn around and the candy is already gone. Peering into the waters below some have actually seen the shadow of a baby.

Decatur 35609

Crybaby Hollow

Another example of a Cry Baby Bridge in a very secluded area off Highway 31 outside of Decatur. You will eventually come to an eight-foot long bridge with no rails that spans a small stream. This location is said to be haunted by the spirit of a crying baby. If you are brave enough to park on the bridge and await the weeping sounds, you might experience the feeling of your car rocking back and forth as though someone is pushing it from side to side. Upon getting out to find out what is going on, you may discover small handprints on the car. So in this case we have a mixture of the Cry Baby Bridge story and the handprint evidence where something is actually said to move the automobile.

Highway 11

A ghost falsely accused of murdering his girlfriend haunts a stretch of the northbound lanes of Hwy 11 and the exit off Hwy 565 between Decatur and Huntsville, Alabama. Lonnie Stephens was convicted of murder in September 1934 but he was completely innocent of the crime but nonetheless sentenced to life in prison. He somehow managed to escape from a chain gang and was hitchhiking along Hwy 11 when he was struck and killed by a car. Many years later the real killer was captured and confessed but it was already too late for Lonnie.

To this very day a ghost is seen standing in the middle of the road pleading with someone to stop, his arms outstretched. Some that do stop do not find anyone there suddenly. He vanishes from sight!

Florence 35633

Ghost Bridge

Florence is a city in and the county seat of Lauderdale County in the northwestern corner of the state. Florence was surveyed for the Cypress Land Company in 1818 by Italian surveyor Ferdinand Sannoner, who named it Florence, the capital of the Tuscany region of Italy. It was incorporated in 1826.

This bridge on the outskirts of Florence is a little hard to reach and very spooky at night. Legends state that a runaway slave was hung from bridge during the time of the Civil War. There have been numerous sightings of the unfortunate slave seen near that bridge since his death.

Another story is told about a battle occurring near that site during the Civil War and later that evening both sides searched for dead and wounded by the light of lanterns. One of the phenomena reported are strange lights moving up and down the banks said to be the soldiers looking for their comrades.

The bridge itself was a large metal structured frame about 25-30 feet tall and one single lane made of wood planks with two rows of planking that you had to keep your tires on. That in itself is scary enough!

Some have seen a rope or something like resembles a rope still hanging from the bridge. To get to the bridge go all the way down the end of Cox Creek Parkway going toward Central and take a right onto "New Savannah Highway/Hwy 20". Go about half a mile and take a right onto the "Old Savannah Highway/CR 200". You'll go about a mile and take a sharp right by an old repair building and you should run right into where the bridge is now closed off. There's a place to turn your car around and get out there.

Gadsden 35901

Pleasant Hill Road Bridge

An infamous legend in the city of Gadsden. A married couple living in a farmhouse nearby got into a bitter argument. The woman ran away with her baby but the gentleman, feeling sorry for his family, got his carriage and began to search for his wife. Hiding near the bridge, the woman appeared out of the bushes and scared the horses so badly that they

knocked both her and the baby into Black Creek where they drowned. Ever since that tragedy, a lady can be observed walking the banks of Black Creek and often carriage wheels can be heard on the wooden bridge even though nothing is visible! A baby's piercing cry also disturbs the silence of the evening.

Hueytown 35023

Lilly Lane

Hueytown is a city in Jefferson County, Alabama. It made international headlines with the unexplainable "Hueytown Hum", a mysterious noise once believed to be related to an underground coal mine in the area. The Hueytown Journal, April 7, 1992, reported that for the past four months the town of Hueytown was plagued by a low-pitched, steady sound emanating from the hills surrounding this coal mining town. The sound kept people awake at night and caused neighborhood dogs to constantly howl. Similar to the sound of a fluorescent light being turned on, theories abounded from killer bees, electromagnetic forces, high-power lines or noises from the mines where numerous people had been killed in the past due to mining accidents.

The mystery was made even more elusive by the fact that one area, with about 500 homes was affected the most. Researchers eventually said they discovered the source and their explanation was "an atmospheric anomaly" involving the interaction of temperature, humidity, barometric pressure, wind and topography that was "propagating, channeling and focusing" the sound to a point miles from the source. Amazing, huh?

Mayor Lillian Howard says she believed the noise came from a huge ventilation fan with 12-foot blades that drives the air out of the mouth of a Jim Walter Resources mine outside Hueytown just west of Birmingham. Not so, said Dennis Hall, spokesman for the coal mining company. So the mystery deepens.

Along sections of Lilly Lane local residents have reported seeing an apparition of an elderly man walking up and down the street at night. He is allegedly dressed in blue jeans and a white shirt and some claim appearances within their own houses! He has been spotted for many years and most believe is a guardian spirit of some kind even though he is unrecognizable.

Jacksonville 36265

Dump Road

Jacksonville is a city in Calhoun County located in eastern Alabama. Jacksonville was founded in 1833 on land purchased from Creek Indian Chief "Du-Hoag" Ladiga. The town was first christened Drayton, but later renamed to honor President Andrew Jackson in 1834.

Dump Road is a local name and cannot be found on any map however it is part of a section of the old Chief Ladiga Indian trail at the base of the foothills of the Appalachian Mountains. It acquired the name Dump Road from all the illegal dumping of garbage by local residents throughout the years. The trail can be found above the unmarked community called "Brownwood Estates."

There was a paved section that was completed going up the hill to the old road that was supposed to be an expansion of that subdivision that was never completed in the 1980s. Allegedly the contractor responsible for developing the property had some kind of bad experience on the road and never completed the subdivision. Today there are poles where power lines would have been laid but no lines are attached to them. It's become a spot for teenagers to frequent at night and four-wheel drive vehicles.

Daytime sightings include reports of horses and wagons making their way up the trail while others report seeing what appears to be a black slave hanging from a nearby tree above a clay embankment which today is used illegally as a shooting range; so beware if you travel that way during the day.

In the late 1980s, a couple who lived nearby hiked into the woods and discovered what could have been an old slave house allegedly where a plantation burned in the early 1990s. Reports from overnight campers are claims of feeling a heavy presence and are often awakened by blood curdling screams in the middle of the night. Others have heard those screams often accompanied by horses galloping and the sounds of an angry mob. Visual encounters of torches and lanterns bobbing about on the trail are all believed to be connected to a possible lynching of slave.

Jasper 35501

Mill Creek Bridge
+33.9.863, -87.28835

Jasper is a city in Walker County Alabama and named in honor of Sergeant William Jasper, a Red Stick War hero. The Creek War fought between 1813-14 was also known as the Red Stick War. The town was settled in 1815 but not incorporated until 1888.

Photo courtesy of James Baughn

Mill Creek Bridge (Camak Bridge) located along Country Club Road just north of the town of Jasper is allegedly haunted by the ghost of a character called Moon Mullins for many years. According to the stories, she died on the bridge under mysterious circumstances over 75 years ago. Since her death, numerous eye witnesses have reported hearing strange noises and seeing apparitions on the bridge as well as the nearby Black Water Creek banks.

Another story is told of the bridge collapsing when two men in an asphalt truck went over it and their ghosts are supposed to haunt the new structure later erected.

Warrior River Bridge
+33.81287, -87.05371

Warrior River Bridge (Dilworth Bridge) located on a private road for the Dilworth Coal Plant is said to be haunted by a man after an eighteen-wheeler struck his car on Warrior River Bridge. The name is being withheld as it cannot be verified, however his ghost now allegedly throws sticks and rocks at other trucks that cross the bridge, venting his anger.

Linden 36748

Sally's Lane

Linden is a city in and the county seat of Marengo County and was originally known as the Town of Marengo but it was later changed to Hohenlinden in 1823 to honor the county's earliest European settlers, French Bonapartist refugees to the Vine and Olive Colony. Hehenlinden was chosen to commemorate Napoleon Bonaparte's battle at Hohenliden, Germany, in which the French were victorious over the Austrians and Bavarians. The spelling was later shorted to Linden.

According to local legends, a young woman was beheaded on this road while riding in her wagon sometime in the 1800s and she still allegedly haunts the lane. A family that owns a campground next to the lane where she was killed has supposedly experienced unexplained events. Green lights and seeing young children in period clothing appearing and disappearing are commonplace along with being physically slapped by something unseen.

Lynn 35575

Highway 5

Lynn is a tiny town in Winston County of less than 600 people and was incorporated in 1952. A story persists to this day of a ghostly woman who haunts a section of Highway 5. She was supposedly walking down the side of Highway 5 near the Winston County Drag Strip when she was struck and killed by an eighteen-wheeler. Her ghost is now said to jump onto the sides of 18-wheelers looking for that hit and run driver that left her for dead

Newton 36352

Choctawhatchee Bridge
+31.34273, -85.61191

Newton is a town in Dale County, Alabama and was once the county seat before 1870 when Ozark took over that distinction. Newton was founded in 1843 after the formation of Coffee County from Dale County's western half, which rendered the original seat of Daleville off-center. The town became a scene for local Confederate recruiting during the Civil War, and was the site of a battle in March 1865 between local Home Guard units and pro-Union irregulars from Florida. The guerillas who sought to burn down the county courthouse were turned back and this event is commemorated by a monument and periodic reenactments.

On December 3, 1864, a local Methodist minister named Bill Sketoe was lynched just north of Newton by local Home Guard troops led by Captain Joseph Brear. Since Sketoe was tall, a hole had to be dug beneath his feet to accommodate his large frame. Local legend tells that the hole that won't stay filled even after being filled in numerous times during the decades that followed. Though covered in 1979 by a new bridge tons of rubble, "Sketoe's hole" still remains a local attraction and was immortalized by Alabama writer Kathryn Tucker Windham in her *13 Alabama Ghosts and Jeffrey*. A monument to Sketoe was dedicated near the hanging site in 2006 and the local museum displays items of Sketoe memorabilia.

The bridge is allegedly haunted by the spirit of Sketoe and local legend states that each of the six vigilantes who partook in the lynching of Sketoe met with violent deaths. Locals report seeing Sketoe's ghost to this day.

The remains of the old wooden bridge can be seen just to the west of the new AL 123 Bridge. A few wooden stubs and a couple of support columns in the river is all that remains of the old wooden bridge.

Opelika 36804

Double Hill Road

Opelika is a city and the county seat in Lee County in eastern Alabama. The first white settlers in Opelika arrived in the later 1830s and established a community called Lebanon. After the removal of the native peoples by force in 1836-37, the area became known as Opelika, taken from a word in the Muskogee language meaning "large swamp." The county of Lee is named for Confederate General Robert E. Lee.

Legend has it that there was an old cemetery said to have been moved years ago. If you can find this very rural road and cross the bridge said to be on this road, just after a few feet beyond the bridge if you look to your right there will be a bright green patch of grass where the cemetery used to be. If you walk down this road late at night, some say at the stroke of midnight, a phantom horseman in a carriage will start coming towards you and then suddenly veer off the road where the old cemetery used to be. If you come back the next day and look around, legend says you will be able to see the tracks where he ran off the road the night before.

Salem-Shotwell Covered Bridge

     The Salem-Shotwell Bridge also known as the Pea Ridge Covered Bridge in Lee County is located halfway down Park Road (formerly the east end of 7th Avenue) at Opelika Municipal Park, which is off North Street, 8.7 miles from Opelika on US 280/431 from I-85. Directions: turn left on Wacoochee School Road, bridge is 1.3 miles farther on the right (32.659294, -85.381372).

     Originally built in 1900 by Otto Puls, the 43-foot bridge is a Town Lattice truss construction over a single span on what is now Shotwell Road (CR 252) just north of the community of Salem. This was about 10 miles east of its current location. Throughout the years high water and erosion from various storms had taken a toll on the old bridge and it was closed to vehicle traffic in 1994 and left to survive the elements.

     In the early morning hours, of June 4, 2005, a severe thunderstorm passed through Lee County and high winds caused a tree to fall on the bridge causing major damage. It eventually collapsed into the Wacoochee Creek later that day. Reconstruction of the bridge began on February 2, 2007 over a section of Rocky Brook and on August 14, 2007 a ribbon-cutting ceremony at Opelika Municipal Park to reopen the bridge was held.

     Legends state that during its time over the Wacoochee Creek, the Salem-Shotwell Covered Bridge was said to have been haunted by children who were killed in a motor vehicle accident near the bridge a number of years ago. No confirmation of any accident was ever found however local police did confirm a strangulation of a girl on the bridge.

There is a famous, oft-told story of leaving candy on the bridge for the dead children and having it disappear. However since the bridge has been moved from its original location to new spot, the hauntings probably have ceased as well.

Saraland 36571

Oak Grove Road

Saraland is a city in Mobile County in the far southern end of Alabama. Present day Saraland was part of a Spanish land grant from Don Diego Alvarez, hence it's original name Alvarez Station. The present name of the city was said to have been given by C.J. DeWitt, a retired minister editor who moved south in 1890 for health reasons.

This story has also been told in nearby Mobile and Satsuma and also surrounds nearby Kali Oka R Road Plantation. On Oak Grove Road there is another so-called Cry Baby Bridge where a woman killed her young child by drowning it in the creek below. Visiting the site day or night, you can hear the sound of a baby crying that appears to be coming from the waters below you.

Talladega 35160

Cemetery Road

Talladega is a city in Talladega County approximately fifty miles east of Birmingham. Talladega is a Muscogee (Creek) Native American word derived from TVLVTEKE.

Cemetery Road is located at 33.435413, -86.126167i in the Talladega National Forest and the houses are widely spaced apart contributing to the foreboding air of the place. Locals claim that if you drive down Cemetery Road at night, the spirits of those buried there will walk the road and become visible to drivers and passengers.

ALASKA

Fairbanks
Chena Hot Springs Road

This road is haunted by ghostly lights. Late at night two lights that resemble headlights seem to follow passing cars. Sometimes it will start to fly and form one bright light. Other times it will look like a fast moving car or truck with bright blue white and orange colored lights. This is a very remote road with no homes or extraneous light sources that could be the possible cause for these lights. Popular natural explanations range from car headlights reflecting off the fallen snow to UFOs.

Only seen in the winter months after 7pm in the sky, these lights sometimes leave trails in the air from their wake.

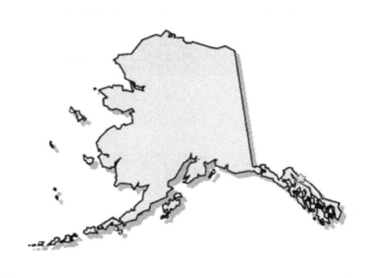

ARIZONA

Fountain Hills 85268
Saguaro Blvd.

Saguaro Blvd. looks like any other ordinary peaceful residential street nestled in a quiet neighborhood however a horrific tale has been told by locals for many years. Allegedly a young girl was kidnapped in the early 1980s and when found was in a horrible condition. She had been murdered and dismembered with some of her body parts found in a home on this otherwise peaceful street.

As people pass by the building after twilight, they may catch a glimpse of an apparition of this little girl standing near the house where she was so brutally murdered. Many times the visual sighting will be accompanied by the sounds of sobbing, crying or even screaming as one might imagine the pain and anguish the girl went through the last moments of her life.

Many, who stop to help out this girl, as she looks like a flesh and blood human, see her disappear in a wink of an eye.

Mesa 85210
8th Avenue

On 8th Avenue in the heart of Mesa the ghost of a little boy has been observed on numerous occasions attempting to cross the road. The child is quite young and observers are worried that he might not make it across the street and that someone should be helping him cross this busy intersection, however by the time the child reaches the center of the street, he completely disappears from sight without a trace.

Allegedly the child was struck and killed by a drunk driver at this location and the ghost, not realizing that he has passed over, continues to try to make it across the street without success.

Phoenix
5th Avenue

On August 6, 1995 a tragic accident occurred on 5th Avenue between Roosevelt and Fillmore where a nine-year-old girl was killed by a hit and run driver and she expired at the scene. Almost immediately afterwards when the ambulances arrived and the body was placed inside for removal, many bystanders insisted that the girl was still alive because they claimed to have seen the face of the girl along with her hands pressed up against the back window of the ambulance as it pulled away.

This was impossible as the paramedics were still attempting to revive the girl in the ambulance at the time. Others say that she was pronounced dead at the scene. But whatever the case whatever many bystanders saw was quite startling and amazing!

Since the accident there have been spotty reports of an apparition of a girl appearing at the site of her demise. Other sightings have occurred near 19th and Camelback. Two young girls were walking home from school one afternoon and encountered this ghost who was walking in front of them, turned, smiled and disappeared.

At the intersection of 51st Street and Indian School Road there is a report of an unhappy female apparition who screams at people as those she's being hit by cars. Residents claim to hear these screams frequently and sometimes the ghost is said to actually enter into nearby homes where she often makes herself quite comfortable on the couch or other times throws household items around.

ARKANSAS

Bono 72416

Bono Bridge

Bono Bridge was built in 1882 and links CR 352 and 353 and is really showing its age. The bridge has been closed for quite some time due to accidents and its unsafe structure. If any bridge looked haunted, this one really fit the bill.

This location is a favorite teen hangout and is known for past satanic rituals that have been performed under the structure. One of the many ghost stories concerns a phantom train that is seen or at least a train light coming down the track towards you very fast. It continues to approach the observer until it just disappears before it actually comes in contact with the bridge or eye witnesses. Others have seen full-bodied apparitions and heard unexplainable noises out there at night. No one seems to know who these apparitions could be unless they are the unfortunate victims of accidents from the past.

Cedarville 72932

Highway 220
At the top of the mountain at Dry Hill Road going north on Highway 220 off the left side of the road is part of the old Butterfield Stage Coach Road people have always reported the sound of someone whistling a strange tune. When they search the surrounding area to make sure its not a joke from someone it always stops when they step onto the Old Stage Coach Road. When the whistling stops you can hear a team of horses running as if the old stagecoach is making another run.

Cotter 72626

Cotter Bridge

Cotter Bridge, also known as the R.M. Ruthven Bridge and the White River Concrete Arch Bridge, was built in 1930 by the Marsh Engineering Company of Des Moines, Iowa. It was officially dedicated on November 30, 1930.

There have been reports of an apparition of a woman being chased by hounds, the sounds of children playing on the train tracks below and even the unearthly sounds of a baby crying. Recently visitors to the bridge and area have heard the distinct sounds of footsteps and have even visually seen the footprints but no real visible person is nearby.

Grant County

Old Redfield Road - Reports of everything and anything, from ghosts wandering the road, apparitions in the cemetery, flashlights and radios going dead with no explanation while in the actual cemetery. An actual experience within the family occurred when driving down the road and the hood of the car flew open for no apparent reason, other than passing the "haunted" cemetery. Upon arriving home, they found nothing wrong with the car that would have caused the hood to unlatch.
Old Redfield Road can be found at 34.310528, -92.386551.

Mena 71953

Billy's Bridge
On nights when the moon is full reports abound of mysterious voices and strange lights that can be seen hovering around the bridge. Not much is known about the history or lore about this place however it is said that rocks and stones will skip across the water without any human intervention.

Paragould 72450

Primrose Lane
Allegedly if you continue to the very end of Primrose Lane where the road turns into a dirt road and travel a bit further down and stop; after shutting off your headlights and waiting for a while an apparition of a man carrying a rifle along with a dog will suddenly appear on the road directly in front of you. Supposedly the man shot himself while hunting and is still

wandering the woods at night. If you are brave enough to approach the ghostly canine, it is said that the animal will come right up to you before vanishing into thin air.

Rogers 72758

Radar Road
Sounds like galloping horses have been heard on or near the road from time to time even though nothing is visibly seen at the time. It has been observed by local residents and other eye witnesses unaware of the story and is thought to date back to the time of the Civil War.

Scott 72142

Mama Lou's Bridge
Another version of a "Cry Baby Bridge." It is said that a woman and her new born baby drove off this bridge and died. If you go there at night and say "Mama Lou I've got your baby" strange things will happen. Your car won't start or you'll hear screeching noises like the paint is being scraped off your car. You can also see a woman in white floating in the field near the bridge.

Springfield 72157

Old Iron Bridge

      Mostly audible sounds can be encountered at this old seldom used bridge. The cries of an infant can be heard but you cannot tell where the sound is coming from. Also a girl screaming bloody murder can be heard as well as other unusual sounds and noises.

Washington 71862

Tily Wily Bridge

Tily Wily Bridge is yet another version of the "Cry Baby Bridge" story and there is mixed versions of the accident story. The first concerns a gentleman falling asleep behind the wheel of his car and driving off the bridge accidentally and drowning himself, his wife and baby. The other story is of a mother who purposely drove off the bridge to commit suicide murder.

Since the accident(s), depending on which story you believe in, the father or mother is seen in a black sedan driving across the bridge and a woman is seen in a white dress twirling in a nearby field. Other reports include visitor's cars dying out for no apparent reason; windows fogging up inside and sometimes the imprints of small baby handprints can be seen. Sounds of a baby crying of course are heard but a more bizarre apparition of a green goblin-like creature has also been seen on the bridge from time to time.

Directions: The best way is heading 540N take the Greenland exit onto "Wilson Road" (turn Right at end of exit). Come to Hwy 71 and turn Left (71 is also "Main St" in Greenland and turns into "School Street" as entering Fayetteville heading North). Turn Right on "Willoughby Road". Turn Right on "S. Wilson Hollow Rd." Follow this little road back until you run into a little narrow concrete bridge. This is *Tilly Willy Bridge*.

Woodson 72180

Woodson-Latteral Road

Hwy 365 several versions of the Vanishing Hitchhiker legend originate on the highways between Little Rock and surrounding communities. Someone picks up a young girl hitchhiking, usually on a rainy night, and when the driver gets to the house where the girl wants to get out she disappears. The astounded driver knocks on the door of the residence only to be told that the ghost of the owner's daughter returns on the anniversary of her death. The girl died in a car wreck at the spot where the driver picked her up. The haunted area on Highway 365 is from Little Rock to Woodson and from Redfield to Pine Bluff.

US Hwy 64 North of Little Rock is the stomping ground of another highway ghost, but this one has a name. Laura Starr Latta died a month before her 20th birthday in an accident on the old road in 1899. The area on U.S. Highway 64 runs from Conway to Morrilton.

The GRS investigated this location on September 14, 1984.

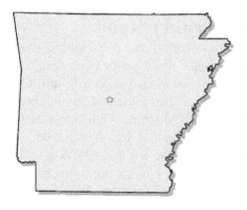

CALIFORNIA

Carson 90745

Alameda & Wilmington Blvd.
A spirit of a man who is dressed in the style of the 1800s has been seen in the area of Alameda and Wilmington/Del Amo Blvd. It has been rumored that when the Dominguez Ranch house was used as a Stage Coach stop over after the Civil War the man was beaten and killed on that area where those streets connect.

Clayton 94517

Morgan Territory Road
Morgan Territory Road is an old logging road that was built back in the 1800's to bring wood from Santa Cruz to the Eastern Contra Costa County, the road cut thru between Livermore and Clayton, since this is a very isolated road there has been a lot that has happen on this road. One of the Legends is of Joaquin Murrieta California Bandit El Dorado; it is believed that Joaquin had buried his loot some where in the Morgan Territory area under an oak tree. In the 1950's a woman and her husband were on there way home from Livermore when they saw a spirit standing next to a oak tree off the side of the road, not knowing the story about the loot at the tree they just thought that they were just seeing things due to the dark of the road and being tired. Once they started letting the story out to their friends and family they found out the story about the loot of Joaquin Murrieta.

From time to time people still report seeing the ghost on Morgan Territory Road but they can never find the spot again when they go back to look for the loot that is believed to be buried there.

El Centro 92243

Dogwood Road

It is said that if you drive along this road after midnight occasionally you will see a girl walking alongside the road. If you stop to give her a ride she will get in, sit down, remain silent and eventually dissipate. However, it is also said that if you do not give her a ride, she will sit on top of your hood and try to make you crash. Stories say she died in a grisly accident along that road.

This is one hitchhiking ghost that you will definitely want to pick up instead of speeding away!

Georgetown 95634

Prospector's Road

This road runs between Georgetown and Lotus, parallel to Marshall Road. It is a treacherous mountain road where dozens of people have died over the last 150 years. Tales are told of a grumpy old prospector who emerges from a patch of weeds on the side of the road. He gradually materializes and floats up the embankment toward oncoming vehicles. He points his finger menacingly and silently mouths "Get off my claim".

Hollywood

Hollywood Blvd.
The intersection of Hollywood Boulevard and Sierra Bonita in Hollywood is steeped in Native American history as there were actual settlements of early Indian settlers. There have been numerous witnesses to seeing phantom Native American Indians riding on horseback and even simulating actual combat such as shooting arrows and hurling tomahawks.

The phantom sounds of Indian drumming have also been reported at this location. This would seem to coincide to historical records indicating that Indians frequently attacked stagecoaches here.

Kern County/Bakersfield

Lerdo Highway
For over a dozen years eye witnesses and motorists have reported seeing an apparition of a women dressed in a flowing white dress in the style of the 1930-40s, floating about a foot off the ground. She always seems to travel east to west on Lerdo Highway between Freeway 99 and State Route 43.

No one seems to know who she is but legend tells us that it was a woman on the way to her wedding when she was killed in a car accident.

Lathrop 95330

Mossdale Bridge
Back in the 1970s, a young man dressed in blue jeans and wearing a red checkered flannel shirt is said to have committed suicide by jumping off the Mossdale Bridge and into the San Joaquin River.

To this day his ghost has been seen around dusk standing on the bridge preparing for his jump into eternity.

Montecito 93108

Ortega Road
The ghosts of 3 nuns allegedly tortured and killed by Indians have haunted this roadway for over 100 years. Las Tres Hermanas, as they have come to be called, stand on the roadside with their arms folded, wearing black and white habits. Ortega road is located in Montecito, which is on Highway 192 in Santa Barbara County.

(National Directory of Haunted Locations, Dennis William Hauck, Penguin Books, ISBN: 0-14-025734-9)

Pasadena

Colorado Street (Suicide) Bridge
The bridge was constructed in 1913 and at least 100 people committed suicide by leaping into the Arroyo Seco from the Colorado Street Bridge by 1939. The bridge was long ago nicknamed the Suicide Bridge and many reports have surfaced that claim the bridge and Arroyo Seco are haunted today by the spirits of those who killed themselves here. The air around the bridge is often described as being "thick". Some people have reported seeing a woman in a flowing robe standing on top one of the bridge's parapets before she leaps over the side and vanishes into thin air. Before the Colorado Street Bridge was even finished one of the workers apparently fell from the height and landed head first into a vat of wet concrete. Other workers assumed he died from the fall and could not be rescued and he was left to die in the quick drying cement and entombed forever. People today sometimes report hearing cries from below the bridge and many think it is the desperate cries of the fallen worker's soul. Other people have reported seeing a man with an old fashioned suit and wire rimmed glasses wandering the bridge. Many have reported strange sounds and cries emanating from around and below the bridge. Animals in the area, including pets walking the bridge and paths below, have been

reported to act strangely in the area constantly looking behind them and eager to move away. Homeless people camping under the bridge have regularly reported seeing ghostly figures and hearing mysterious noises. On May 1, 1937 a despondent mother reportedly threw her baby over the side of the bridge before leaping to her own death. Miraculously the baby landed in the thick branches of a tree and survived.

The bridge was designed and built by the J.A.L. Waddel firm of Kansas City, Missouri and named for Colorado Street, which was the major east-west thoroughfare through the Pasadena area. The first suicide occurred on November 16, 1919 and was followed by a number of others, especially during the Great Depression. The bridge is listed on the National Register of Historic Locations.

Salinas 93901

Old Stage Road
Old stage road has been known for many hauntings. It runs right outside of Salinas and goes through the back roads of King City. One of the most infamous stories that have been passed down was back in the late 1800's or early 1900's there was a woman that was walking along side the road and there was a man who asked her for a ride and she accepted it. After a couple of minutes passed by, he pulled over and savagely attacked and raped her. After this horrendous act he took the body out into the fields and decapitated her. Then he went out threw the head into the fields and left the body. After that there were sightings of a woman walking down the road holding her own head or you see a woman walking and if someone picks her up she'll sit there for a moment and then vanishes right where the crime occurred.

(Shadowlands Website: www.theshadowlands.net)

San Diego

Cabrillo Bridge

The Cabrillo Bridge was built for the Panama-California Exposition of 1915. Building began in 1912 under the supervision of Frank P. Allen Jr. The bridge was designed by Thomas B. Hunter of San Francisco and it was officially dedicated on April 12, 1914 by Franklin D. Roosevelt, then Secretary of the Navy.

The Cabrillo Bridge is located off the 163 Freeway in San Diego. It has also acquired the nickname Suicide Bridge over the years. Many people who have walked over the bridge have felt an uneasy feeling including Nicole Strickland, Southern California Research Assistant for the GRS. An apparition of an old man has been seen in and around the bridge only to suddenly disappear and reappear in another location.

(Field Guide to Southern California Hauntings, Nicole Strickland, GRS Press, ISBN: 978-0-9797115-4-1)

Coronado Bridge

The Coronado Bridge connects San Diego with the community of Coronado. It crosses right over San Diego Bay. The construction of the bridge started in February of 1967 and was opened on August 3, 1969 during a celebration honoring the 200th Anniversary of the founding of San Diego. It has been known as the 3rd deadliest bridge in the United States as many people have taken their lives by jumping off the high structure. Thus, there is no doubt that this bridge may have residual haunting effects. It has been said that 200+ suicides have occurred on the Coronado Bridge.

(Nicole Strickland, Southern California Area Research Assistant for the GRS)

San Francisco

California Street
California Street is located in the Nob Hill district of San Francisco. The ghost of a woman dressed in a Victorian era dress has been

known to haunt this street for a very long time. Apparently, many feel that the female apparition is that of Flora Sommerton. Apparently, Sommerton ran away in 1876 instead of consenting to an arranged marriage.

Eventually her body was found in Butte, Montana where she was working as a housekeeper under an assumed name, Mrs. Butler. The room where her body was found was filled with newspaper articles concerning her disappearance and at the time of her death she was wearing her bridal gown. Nowadays people still see her ghost walking up and down California Street.

(Supernatural California, Preston Dennett)

Golden Gate Bridge

The bridge is part of Route 101 and 1 and it bridges together San Francisco with Marin County. It was completed in 1937 and was the longest suspension bridge in the world when its completion was finished. It is one of the most famous landmarks of California and San Francisco and is a favorite among many people.

On a more tragic side, the Golden Gate Bridge is also the site of many suicides. Apparently, it is the most well-liked places to commit suicide in the US and even the world. By 2005, the number of suicides reached an excess of 1,200 and averaged 1 suicide every two weeks. Those that do survive the fall from the bridge usually die from drowning or freezing to death as the water temperature is quite cold. In October of 2008, the Golden Gate Board of Directors voted to construct a plastic-covered steel net to be placed below the bridge as a suicide prevention measure.

With all this negative and despondent residual energy from all those who took their lives, is it any wonder that this is the most haunted bridge anywhere in the world?

San Juan Capistrano 92675

Los Rios Street

Los Rios Street is located in San Juan Capistrano and near the San Juan Capistrano Mission. Los Rios Street may in fact house the most paranormal activity in the area and areas alongside the are also reported to be haunted, such as the former Albert Pryor House, Rios Adobe and Montanez Adobe.

There is a portion of the road that lays alongside the railroad tracks. Local legend claims that this exact area is home to the phantom named "The White Lady of Capistrano." This female specter was possibly a witch back when she was alive and fell in love with a man living in the 19th century.

According to one legend, this woman poisoned herself to death on the porch of this same man. This ghost has been seen appearing out of a white fog, walking alongside the railroad tracks. She is sometimes noticed with the phantom spirit of a black dog who is purported to spit fire.

(Field Guide to Southern California Hauntings, Nicole Strickland, GRS Press, ISBN: 978-0-97997115-4-1)

Ortega Highway

Construction of this highway began in 1929 and lasted through 1933 as a way to bridge Lake Elsinore with San Juan Capistrano. The highway's name honors Don Jose Francisco Ortega who was a member of the Portola expedition. Along with his father, Ortega made the very first attempt to found the Mission San Juan.

The highway was the original site of Indian foot paths and a fire trail.

Directions: I-15 to Lake Elsinore, west of Central Ave, turn right; turn left on Riverside Drive, the road curves into Grand Ave.; follow Grand Ave. to a 3-way stop and turn right onto 74 Ortega Highway.

Santa Clara County

Pacheco Pass

Psychic Sylvia Brown has described this stretch of highway as being quite horrific. I had a chance to meet Ms. Brown in person on a live NBC television show *The Other Side* a number of years ago. I was talking about my experiences at Spooklight Road in Joplin, Missouri and she was relating the many frightening encounters in Pacheco Pass. During her visit with the camera crew, even the equipment failed a few times mysteriously!

Many people have reported odd and scary experiences on Pacheco Pass, some seeing the apparitions of Indians, wagons and soldiers. This pass is one of the most fatal roads in California.

Apparently, Pacheco Pass somehow caused unexplained feelings of paranoia and violence among its drivers. Sensitives have reported feelings of panic and dread on the highway and clairvoyants have had visions of Indians and pioneer settlers fighting amongst themselves.

(Supernatural California, Preston Dennett)
(Weird California by Greg Bishop, Joe Oesterle & Mike Marinacci)

Stockton 95202

Eight Mile Road

On the east side of Highway 99, drivers may encounter a woman all dressed in white standing on the side of the road and sometimes that same woman will be seen in the rearview mirror sitting in the backseat of their automobile.

Another apparition of a young Indian girl seen sporting a load of jewelry has been seen in broad daylight at the intersection of Eight Mile road before simply disappearing into nothingness.

(Shadowlands Website: www.theshadowlands.net)

West Hollywood

Laurel Canyon Blvd.

This street separates the areas of West and North Hollywood and is reportedly quite haunted. The haunted area is located at Lookout Mountain approximately a mile down the south area where a traffic light exists. People who have driven through this exact area have said that at midnight, a phantom carriage with white horses have been seen only to disappear a few seconds later.

(Supernatural California, Preston Dennett)

COLORADO

Aurora

Third Bridge #2

Travel east on Smokey Hill Rd and take a left at the stop sign when the road becomes one lane each way. Drive all the way up and down over the hills on the dirt road until you come to the third bridge. Local High School students have died there in a car accident. Drums can be heard in the distance and if people visiting the bridge are loud and obnoxious, the drums get louder and closer as though whomever playing them wants you to hear. It is said that an Indian massacre took place there in which settlers killed the men in battle and then returned and killed the woman and children of the tribe. Some have reported fog rolling in from both directions and have seen a man floating on a horse and other strange things.

(Shadowlands Website: www.theshadowlands.net)

Bennett 80102

Train Bridge over Kiowa Creek

A great many years ago there was a tragic train crash (according to legend) and many people were killed on or near this bridge. To this very day at night you can hear the sound of train whistles approaching in the distance; thought to be the sounds of the phantom train.

Thornton 80020

Riverdale Road

Riverdale Road is a very long strip of dirt road that is very dark. It is said that it was all farmland in the 1700 - 1800's. This is a location of slavery abuse, witchcraft and hangings. There is a small turn off road at about 132nd where the cornfields are high and the oil mills are silent. When you park your car on this gravel road and turn the car off and roll your windows down, you can hear the pace of someone running down this road and passing your car. You can also feel a presence there that makes you want to hide. If you listen carefully you can also hear the sound of screams and a faint heart beat that slowly gets louder and louder until you feel the need to cover your ears. You can only take so much of this before you have to turn the car on and take off!

When driving down Riverdale road, there has been sightings of a women dressed in white waiting at the side of the road, if you pull up to her it is said that she walks to your car but disappears before getting in.

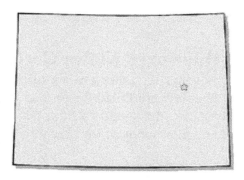

CONNECTICUT

Kensington 06037

Chamberlain Highway

Along Rt. 72, Chamberlain Highway in the spring and fall of every year it is said that coyotes can be heard yelping in the distance for about five minutes and then dead silence until one hears the faint sounds of a trumpet being blown. Legend says that back in the 1800s at Ragged Mountain a young boy got lost in the woods and the coyotes probably got to him one night. The trumpet that people have been hearing all these years is probably the boy's last ditch effort in getting help before being devoured by the wildlife.

Torrington 06790

Oak Avenue

This street is haunted by the ghost of a little girl allegedly killed in the 1950s in a wooded area approximately a mile or so from Rt. 8. When she is seen, she is carrying a dog collar and often wearing a long white shredded dress. Many local residents have reported seeing her on foggy full moon nights wandering and crying along the road. According to local reports, winter seems to be the best time to see her. Witnesses claim when they attempt to approach her, she simply vanishes from sight!

DELAWARE

Frederica 19946

Highway 12W

A man, quite angry with his landlord, murdered the landlord then ground him up with cornmeal. He then fed it to his dog. It is said that the phantom dog with its red, glowing eyes can be seen by drivers at night along the side of the road.

Newark

Cooch's Bridge

The battle of Cooch's Bridge was a Revolutionary War engagement between the Colonists lead by General George Washington and the British and Hessian troops under Generals Cornwallis, Howe and Knyphausen and was fought on September 3, 1777. It was the only battle fought on Delaware soil and the first one where the Stars and Stripes waved in battle. Many believe that this was a delaying battle to prevent Cornwallis from taking Philadelphia. However, greatly outmanned and outgunned, the colonists were driven back and Philadelphia eventually fell on September 11th after he defeated the colonists in the Battle of Brandywine.

One of the many stories told is of a British soldier that had his head shot off during the battle and it is said that the specter of that soldier can still be seen on foggy nights walking the roads in the area.

Salem Church Road

In the 1900's, a family of six was hung due to accusations of witchcraft. This family has been seen, all six of them, walking along this highway, in search, people say, of the relatives who hung them.

FLORIDA

Daytona Beach

Orange Avenue Bridge

At the northeast side approach of the bridge many have seen the apparition of a woman in a night robe. Nobody seems to know who she is but since there is water nearby it seems likely that the woman died an unfortunate death of drowning. Objects like chairs and such have been seen flying about as if thrown but there is no wind blowing at the time!

Gainesville 32601

Williston Road

Located somewhere near Gainesville and perhaps down Williston Road out beyond the city limits, a strange light was first reported there in the late 1950s or early 1960s.

Back before the encroachment of urban sprawl and its artificial lights, the county roads in central Florida could get very dark on moonless nights. It was on one such night that a man was driving home rather late. It was warm, and he had his driver-side window down, his left arm resting along the edge as he drove. After a few miles, he saw a single light coming towards him, close to the dividing line in the middle of the road. As dark as it was, he couldn't actually see the vehicle, but he assumed it was a motorcycle. It wasn't. it was actually a semi-truck whose driver was either drunk or asleep at the wheel – its left headlight was burned out, so all the man saw was the right headlight as the truck barreled down the middle of the road and plowed into him,

The man was killed instantly. The arm he'd had resting in the window was severed and flung into the woods, and one of the headlights was knocked clear of the wreckage. Later, officials at the scene of the crash searched and searched for the arm and the headlight, but neither was ever recovered.

That's the background. Now if you drive out to that lonely stretch of road on moonless nights and park your car over on the shoulder and wait, eventually you'll see a light. One such report came from a couple who decided to see if the stories were indeed true. They went out there as a prank and saw a light way off in the distance, and gradually it got closer and closer until it seemed to literally touch their windshield and vanish.

They say it's the accident victim out with the headlight that the police never found still searching for his missing arm!

Jacksonville

Ghost Light Road

Located in extreme NE Florida at the junction of I-10 and I-95 in St. John's County, Greenbrier or Ghost Light Road runs east off Hwy 13 about 7 miles south of the Duval County Line.

This mysterious ball of concentrated light called the "Greenbrier Light," seems to be attracted to moving objects. Cars moving slowing down the road in either direction bring out the light, which follows between 25 to 300 feet behind. Occasionally the light moves over the cars, but it never passes them. In 1987, the St. John's Sheriff's Department asked several scientists to investigate the phenomenon, but no definite conclusion as to the source of the light could be reached. According to local legend, the light is the headlight of a phantom motorcycle. A young man was supposedly pushing his new motorcycle to maximum speed on the road when he lost control and hit the support cable of a telephone pole. His decapitated body was found the next day.

(Source: National Directory of Haunted Places by Dennis William Hauck)

Lady Lake 32158

Rolling Acres Road
All up and down this road just outside of town reports have circulated of extremely loud roars, yells and screams that apparently come out of nowhere.

There are also a numerous eye witnesses to an apparition of a lady dressed in white said to be very "bright" that walks up and down this road in the middle of the night. Some say her name is Julia and that she was murdered by an unidentified man while waiting to get married.

Marianna 32446

Bellamy Bridge

This is a sad tale of a ghost of a woman named Elizabeth Jane Bellamy that roams the swamps of the Chipola River near Marianna. The bridge is extremely hard to get to being that it is on private property but the river is part of public state canoeing trails and that is one legal way of visiting this location.

Elizabeth was the wife of Dr. Samuel C. Bellamy, a politician and examiner of Florida's Union Bank. There were to be married but tragedy struck and that never happened. Depending on which story is told, Elizabeth was either lounging or dancing when her dress caught fire from the nearby fireplace and she ran screaming from the house. Before the fire could be put out, she was terribly burnt and later died and was buried in the family cemetery very close to the modern day Bellamy Bridge.

Soon after her death, a spectral figure of a lady dressed in a long gown, thought to be that of Elizabeth, was spied near the riverbanks on numerous occasions.

GEORGIA

Bartow County

Hardin Bridge

A number of years ago it is said that a couple driving across this bridge saw the oncoming lights of another car approaching them rather quickly. Rather than depressing the accelerator or backing up, they decided to make a turn on the bridge and accidentally drove their vehicle completely off the bridge into the waters below.

If you walk across the bridge at night, you can sometimes hear voices and screams perhaps those of the hapless couple and their unfortunate accident. Some even claim to get about halfway across the bridge when they suddenly see a pair of headlights quickly approaching them. However the car or whatever it is never makes the bridge but hits the bank on the other side.

Clarksville 30523

Canon Bridge

Allegedly there was an argument between a husband and a wife on this bridge and the husband threw his wife over the bridge in a fit of rage. If you wish to witness the ghostly phenomena, return to the bridge on the night between April 12th and 14th and sit on the bridge in your car with your lights off. Suddenly the bridge will be covered in fog and the couple will be heard arguing followed by a loud splash in the water.

On many occasions the ghost of the dead wife has allegedly walked up towards the windows of parked automobiles while others driving across the bridge has their car suddenly die without any valid explanation.

The bridge is actually closer to the town of Demorest on Hwy 115/Canon Bridge Road. Apparently a new bridge was built and opened in October of 2003. Most of the old bridge is gone today.

Colquitt 39837

White's Bridge Road

Around twilight people have seen the apparition of a black man walking eastbound on Mason Road which runs parallel with White's Bridge Road. Apparently this apparition has some connection to the apparitions seen at White's Bridge Road.

The Spring Creek flows underneath White Bridge at the southeast portion of the bridge. Below is a small church and cemetery which has seen its share of erosion from the creek receding and rising year after year. Headstones can be seen in the river itself; a testament to that erosion. Due to that many reports of strange sounds and unexplainable lights have been seen from the bridge looking down towards the church and cemetery. Perhaps those unfortunate whose bodies were washed away are still restless today and trying to find their way back to their rightful resting place.

On the bridge itself, an apparition of a woman has been seen walking often accompanied by the constant crying of a baby or young child.

Columbus

Crybaby Bridge

The same story is told here of either a woman purposely or accidentally drowning her baby in the waters below on the third bridge in the woods on Whitesville Road.

People that come to the bridge to hear the baby crying often turn off their cars to silence the noise, only to notice that they have a problem getting them started again. Besides the sound of a baby crying, a figure in white is seen walking through the woods near the bridge.

Newnan 30263

Cedar Creek Bridge

The current Cedar Creek Bridge on Roscoe Road in Coweta County which spans Cedar Creek is actually a replacement of the original one. Back in the 1930s allegedly a horrible accident involving a women and her child occurred there making the bridge a haunted hangout for ghost investigators and teenagers alike.

The apparition of the woman has been seen and heard there over the decades in various ways, shapes, forms and sounds. Other manifestations include extreme temperature drops and a ghost car that has been seen in the area.

Valdosta 31606

Spook Bridge

The bridge that spans the Withlacoochee River is host to a number of urban legends and teenage fantasies. The bridge was probably built in the late teens or early 1920s according to electrical superintendent of Quitman, Charles Arnold. The land was originally owned by the Cunningham family including the Blue Springs Resort that was once across the bridge near the train stop.

According to Larry Cunningham, nephew of the late Walter Cunningham who used to own the property, a tragic crash occurred on the bridge in the mid-1940s. A truck loaded with gas crashed on the Brooks County side of the bridge and tore out almost 100 feet of the railing which was never replaced.

There were at least two drownings nearby at a location called Blue Hole before 1970. Swimmers diving off the large Cypress tree overlooking the Blue Hole have sometimes missed the hole and hit the surrounding area which is only approximately four feet deep.

There has been an influx of satanic into the area with the inscription of symbols and such on the bridge and this was when the bridge got its name Spook Bridge.

A doctor of Sociology says that she has heard a number of supernatural tales associated with the bridge in the past including that of a man that lived in a nearby house that apparently went crazy and killed his wife. Allegedly he or she haunts the bridge. Another version of the story states that the same couple living there was walking the bridge one evening when he suddenly pushed her off the bridge to her death and she has been seen forever trying to climb up out of the water.

According to a Brooks County Sheriff, a murder even occurred there in the past where a man was shot off the bridge, twice in the head; execution style.

White County (Cleveland)

Stovall Covered Bridge

This is the smallest covered bridge in the state of Georgia and built in 1895, it is one span of thirty-three feet long made up entirely of wood. It spans Chickamauga Creek in White County and is currently owned by the White County Historical Society.

The bridge once served as the link from Cleveland to Clayton Road but by 1959 the road was moved. This bridge was featured in the 1951 movie *"I'd Climb the Highest Mountain"* by Rory Calhoun.

The supernatural occurrences on this bridge are all auditory and come in the form of the crying of unseen babies and the sounds of horse drawn carriages making their way across the bridge however nothing is ever visually seen.

HAWAII

Honolulu

Highway 1

H-1 or Highway 1 is the busiest interstate highway in the state of Hawaii. It is located on the island of O'ahu and is always sometimes referred to as the Lunalilo Freeway. West of Middle Street, H-1 is also known as Queen Lili 'uokalani Freeway. It is the westernmost and southernmost interstate highway in the United States.

Many call this highway one of the most haunted places on the islands. When digging through the mountains it was said that some workers saw Hawaiian spirits that frightened some off the work place. Bones of the dead were also allegedly found in the mountains during construction. It took many years to build this highway due to trying to find the necessary manpower that weren't afraid or superstitious of the old Hawaiian legends. Some say that even today when you drive through the mountains, you can hear the cries from the old ancient Hawaiians.

Nu'uanu

Old Pali Highway

Motorists traveling along this highway have allegedly seen a very large ghostly white blob traversing across the road in front of their vehicles as they drive towards the Pali Lookout at night.

There have been numerous accidents out on this stretch of road so caution is advised if you decide to visit this location. Even the light from the full moon can often be blocked by the forest.

IDAHO

Caldwell 83605

River Road Bridge

Allegedly a long time ago, a woman hung herself from this bridge and when people drive out there at night and turn off their car lights just before crossing the bridge, they will sometimes see her shadow on the side of the bridge.

You can also hear splashes in the water from time to time as there have been other suicides of people jumping to their death from this bridge.

Eye witnesses also claim to see a strange ghost light on the island every night at 7pm but there is no house or buildings out there to cast a light. It's a weird unexplainable event.

ILLINOIS

Algonquin 60102

Square Barn Road

This lonely stretch of roadway is host to several apparitions that have been seen throughout the years. Usually the scenario begins when suddenly two kids run across the street in front of an approaching automobile almost hitting them with the vehicle. They are then sometimes pursued by three others; two boys and a girl running after them. Supposedly there was a murder of two youngsters in the past by these three and what people are seeing is a ghostly reenactment of that event.

The GRS investigated this location on July 21, 2007.

Barrington 60010

Cuba Road

Cuba Road is located between Barrington Road and Old Barrington Road in Barrington however the haunted section seems to be closest to a small cemetery, White Cemetery.

On foggy nights the near curve in road a man's figure will step out suddenly in front of a car. Driver feels contact of something with the car but when he gets out to check, there is nothing on the road and nothing on the car. There have been multiple witnesses to strange ghost lights often described as red to white in color hovering or drifting into and out of the cemetery after dusk. Legend says that a woman was also killed on horseback and that her ghost can be seen, horse and all. Animals in the form of ghostly cows have been reported along Cuba Road fronting the cemetery.

A fascinating account describes two apparitions seen walking hand in hand along Cuba Road across from the cemetery. Every November the shadows of these two are seen walking along the roadside until they turn into another street and vanish from site. The apparitions aren't actually seen but only the shadows they cast on the road. This is a rare daytime sighting here at White Cemetery.

Further down Cuba Road at the intersection of the Northwest Highway is a set of railroad tracks that apparently has been the scene of a phantom train. Motorists at night will see an approaching train light in the distance and wonder why the crossing gates aren't coming down. They sometimes stop their vehicles, get out and look up the tracks only to see nothing there!

The GRS investigated this location on December 11, 1993.

Rainbow Road

Allegedly down Rainbow Road where Kaitlin's Way is now located used to be an old insane asylum. People claim to hear the sounds and screams from the patients very near the driveway to old asylum.

Also near the intersection of Cuba and Rainbow Road many years ago an old mansion burnt to the ground under mysterious circumstances. Even today, people believe that they can still catch a glimpse of that house sometimes engulfed in flames or seen through waves and waves of heat generated by the fire that destroyed the home.

Reports of some satanic rituals and activity in the past have also been reported in the woods around the area.

Benton 62812

Cry Baby Bridge

Another version of the Cry Baby Bridge story where a mother threw her baby over the bridge and into the water to drown. The sounds of a baby crying at night can be heard echoing throughout the general area. This location is quite remote with no houses anywhere nearby that could be the source of this sound.

Just a bit further up this road as you head back towards the main highway, people have caught a glimpse of a phantom house that appears and disappears from time to time. Not much is known about the circumstances surrounding this building or its occupants but its similar to stories told at Bachelor's Grove Cemetery of a disappearing structure.

The GRS investigated Benton August 18, 2007.

Burr Ridge 60521

German Church Road

German Church Road was named after the Trinity Lutheran Church that served the original German immigrants in the area. It became known locally in 1957 as the place where the bodies of Barbara and Patricia Grimes were found.

Barbara and Patricia Grimes, 15 and 13 years of age, respectively had left home about 7:30 p.m. December 26, 1956 for the Brighton Theater at 4223 Archer Avenue to see an Elvis Presley movie, "Love Me Tender." The girls never stayed out past midnight so Mrs. Loretta Grimes was frantic around 2:15 a.m. when she telephoned the Brighton Park police station to report that her teenage daughters had not returned home yet.

On January 23, 1957, nearly a month after the disappearances, a passing motorist, Leonard Prescott of Hinsdale, Illinois was driving on German Church Road when he noticed something unusual in a culvert by Devil's Creek, a small tributary of the Des Plaines River. He stopped and looked down in the culvert and approximately thirty feet above Devil's Creek he saw what looked like two nude bodies. He assumed they were discarded clothing-store dummies.

He drove home and told his wife who insisted they go back to the scene to make sure of what he saw. They both made the grisly discovery of the Grimes sisters, unceremoniously thrown into a ditch. They immediately called the Bedford Park police station. The searching was over.

A real ghost has been seen on German Church Road near the guardrails that mark the location where the bodies were found. In fact it is a ghostly reenactment of the dumping of the bodies. For those people living nearby it's been a common occurrence to hear the sounds of a car screeching to a halt in front of the guardrails in the dead of night. They hear the car open its doors, something landing in the weeds, the doors shut and then the car peeling away.

On several occasions a car was visible as well as the ghostly sounds and a local resident called the Cook County police and stated that she had seen a grisly apparition. Although the vision was hazy and not perfect, she saw what appeared to be a car looking like a black sedan unloading two nude bodies over the side of the guardrails before disappearing. And on rare occasions both the sights and sounds are experienced.

The GRS investigated German Church Road on August 8, 1992.

Byron 61010

Kennedy Hill Road

A mysterious lady in white was first seen in this most rural town just before Christmas of 1980. Scores of onlookers, sometimes bumper to bumper, flocked to the area like so many pigeons. They were attempting to catch a glimpse of a slender young woman allegedly wearing little clothing seen wandering Kennedy Hill Road near Short even in sub-freezing weather.

One man who says he saw the woman is Dave Trenholm who was twenty-five at the time. Trenholm was driving with Guy Harriett of Oregon about 9 PM on January 2nd 1981. He told Chicago Tribune reporter Mary Elson, "She stepped out from behind some bushes by the side of the road. At first it didn't register. I thought it was a deer or a dog. I slammed on the brakes because I was afraid it would dart out into the road."

When he finally realized what it was, he couldn't believe his own eyes. His description of the woman was "tall, slender, and nice-looking, about 20. All she was wearing were some black panties and some kind of scarf around her neck." The temperature that evening was around 10 degrees. She ran towards and then behind a nearby farmhouse and disappeared. They thought about going after her but thought twice in case it was a "sucker trap".

Theories abound including the possibility of it being a retarded girl in her early twenties who was reported missing by her parents in Oregon around Christmas time. Others believe in may be a car accident victim still wandering the site where she perished. Persons who have seen her speculate she is a ghost from an abandoned graveyard on Kennedy Hill Road that has been plowed over.

Additional sightings continued through the middle of January including many who saw the strange woman in light-colored shorts and sweatshirt or shorts and a light jacket. Then she was seen in shorts and a halter-top. Remember this is in the dead of winter on a lonely country farm road with neighbors located quite far apart. No other cars were seen in the vicinity of any sightings nor were any other persons on foot.

In late January 1980 the *Rockford Register Star* ran an article that the mysterious lady was run over by an Ogle County Sheriff's squad car around 8 PM. Not only did the squad car run over her but also the deputies could actually hear her bones crunch as the tires of their vehicle drove over her body. However, when they got out investigating, there was no body or woman there!

A police Lieutenant called the story crazy and untrue but still the stories and sightings persist. So, I decided to go there with *Rockford Register Star* reporter Neal Justin in May of 1992. I wanted to see the terrain for myself and examine possible hiding places and rule out the possibility of optical illusions.

We interviewed actual eyewitnesses who had come into direct contact with the mysterious lady and were told other encounters not reported in the various articles that came out in 1980 and 1981. We didn't see the ghost but it had been over eleven years since the stories began. Maybe she's just lying dormant for a while and will someday reappear!

The GRS investigated Byron May 15, 1992.

Cherry Valley 61016

Bloods Point Road

Bloods Point Road is one of these obscure places that are fancifully mixed with urban legends, lore and maybe some real events. Which is which is however anyone's guess. The road and perhaps the property were from the family name Blood; Arthur Blood being the matriarch of the family.

Some of the weird things reported in the past have included a phantom pick-up truck and semi, and a vanishing patrol car. As many as eight people have allegedly hung themselves from the railroad bridge; one of those include a witch and even Arthur Blood himself! Some even claim that an entire school bus loaded with children plummeted from the bus killing them all.

Mysterious red lights are said to dance around the intersection of Blood Point and Sweeney and an apparition of an old farmer has been seen in that area chasing people off the property with a shotgun in his hand! Some of the reports are connected with someone called Witch Beulah that supposedly lived in the area.

One thing to remember if you visit this area, the police frequently patrol this area issuing tickets for late nighters.

Chicago

49th & Loomis 60609

Headless horsemen ghosts are almost a staple in New England states especially since the writing of Washington Irving's novel, *The Legend of Sleepy Hollow*. Headless riders on horseback would surely be enough to scare most in literature but encountering them in real-life is terrifying!

Near 49th Street and Loomis is where local residents have seen headless horsemen. The viaduct nearby is allegedly haunted by a dark, shadowy figure on horseback minus his head! At least two good, first-hand accounts of this story have come forth and related this tale and possibly more.

On July 7, 1894 the famous south side railroad riots took place right at this viaduct. It was here that the National Guards set up a command post and riflemen to shoot down on people who were protesting the railroads at that time. This was a labor dispute that reached almost mammoth proportions and a series of deaths were attributed to the violence of the time.

There was actually a Calvary encampment very nearby and troops on horseback were used in riot control. When the crowd failed to disperse the troops initially charged with fixed bayonets, and then was ordered to shoot at will. Four people were killed and twenty were seriously injured. Four soldiers and a lieutenant were also wounded where the headless horsemen is said to haunt. Many would argue that there seems to be no reason to doubt this story historically.

Death Alley 60601

The former Iroquois Theater in Chicago now called the Oriental (Ford Center for the Performing Arts) was the scene of the worse theater fire in US history. On December 30, 1903, Mr. Bluebird was scheduled to be played in this theater which should never have been allowed to be opened. There were many major fire hazards that were overlooked or fire inspectors were simply paid off in an effort to open the theater early. Exit doors were covered by draperies, theater doors opened inward instead of outward, the fire escape ladders weren't functional, ventilation doors in the ceiling did not open, and people were literally padlocked into their section by gates to prevent show goers from switching seats in the middle of a performance.

When the main stage curtain caught on fire, instead of evacuating the theater, they continued to perform while off-stagehands tried to fight the fire. The asbestos fire-proof curtain did not fully deploy and when they finally got some ventilation doors open, a serious back draft created a huge fireball that roared into the lower level of the theater, killing many instantly!

Some tried to use the fire escape ladders in the alley of the theater but soon learned that they did not deploy. Faced by the prospect of burning to death or taking a chance to jump to safety, many chose to jump from the great height instead. The first to jump probably died on impact. Those who survived the fall were most likely killed by others who fall upon them. Firefighters estimate as many as 150 people were piled up in Death Alley. The final death toll was over 600 dead!

Many walking past or through the alley since that disaster that felt an uncomfortable presence and great grief and sadness. Others have smelled the odor of burning building. Could it be that those unfortunate victims still linger there to this very day?

The GRS investigated this location on March 28, 2009.

Marquette Road & Ashland Ave. 60645

In 1965, a former Geography teacher was walking on 67th Street just west of Western Avenue with four friends when suddenly a gray-greenish glow began walking toward them. It took the shape of a man, and they could see right thru him. When he came closer, his face appeared to glow.

This frightened them so much, they ran. The figure ran too, but the other way. When they looked back, it was gone and they were glad of it. The figure apparently never returned.

There were no further reports of this strange figure since 1965 even though reliable witnesses reported it.

Sheridan Road (Calvary Cemetery)

Cemeteries can both be beautiful and picturesque at the same time Calvary is both of that. Calvary is situated along Sheridan Road within lapping distance of Lake Michigan the elaborate limestone gates designed by noted architect, James Egan. Consecrated in 1859, it is one of the oldest cemeteries in the Chicagoland area. Many of graves in Calvary however are much older due primarily to the fact that a great deal of burials in Lincoln Park was moved here when that location ceased being a cemetery.

The ghost of Calvary Cemetery is not someone who is buried in the cemetery but someone who is trying to get in. The apparition is described as a figure of man, dripping wet and in some cases seaweed strewn crawling or weaving through the traffic along Sheridan Road. He is apparently trying to enter the cemetery. Locals have dubbed him *Seaweed Charlie* and he has been seen for quite a number of years.

Many possible explanations for the identity of the ghost abound including that FH-1 Phantom from nearby Glenview Naval Air Station crashed into the lake very near Northwestern University on May 4, 1951. The instructor drowned before help could arrive to rescue him and his body was later discovered on the rocks adjacent to the cemetery.

Certainly this is a ghost we can feel for. Who wants to be forever floating in Lake Michigan? He apparently prefers the consecrated grounds of the cemetery to the cold water. The assistant sexton at the cemetery just laughs about the legend and is quoted as saying, "I've been (sic) years but I've never heard of any *Seaweed Charlie*". And then there's the knowledge that Lake Michigan doesn't contain any seaweed. However the sexton isn't a total skeptic, "Maybe it's actually alewives or algae," he offered.

Suicide Bridge (old Lincoln Park Lagoon)

This marvel of a bridge spanning the Lincoln Park Lagoon was built in 1894 and arched 42 feet at its highest point over the water. People came from near and far to see the sights while others had a more sinister plan in mind; ending their lives. Just a half-dozen years later or so policeman who often patrolled this bridge were well aware of the many so-called ghost stories of those unfortunate leapers.

Nobody seems to know just how many people actually committed suicide here but surely the number must be close to 100 or more with quite a number that did not succeed in taking their life.

Some of the headlines from newspapers at the time include: *Policeman Spoils a Suicide: Interferes When Fascinated Crowd in Lincoln Park is Waiting for Man to Kill Self* and *Jumps from Bridge: Says he Tried Suicide for Fun* were just some of the man reports from this bridge that eventually closed in 1919 as it was in terrible condition and deemed unsafe.

Collinsville

Lebanon Road (Gates of Hell)

This is one of the craziest stories I've heard concerning roads or bridges (gates). Lebanon Road has been dubbed by locals the Gates of Hell and I believe it's more a test of manhood than it is a ghost story or urban legend. There is a specific route that you must start from and drive through and under these underpasses in a certain order otherwise and you don't pass under the same one twice, at the stroke of midnight as you drive through the last gate, you will be plucked out of your car and ported to hell. Quite an imagination!

Another tale relates that if you sit under any of these and turn your headlights out, the spirits will send out fiendish hell hounds to bring back your soul; but it doesn't say from where.

To reach these (gates) follow these directions, if you dare:

1. Take West Main Street in Collinsville, Illinois – East - to Lebanon Road and turn left. Keep traveling it till your out of town and soon you'll come upon Gate #1.

2. Shortly after Gate #1 Lebanon Road will turn to the right, but you need to turn immediately to the left onto Lockman Road and smack into Gate #2.

3. Go through Gate #2 and keep following Lockman Road. You'll come to a place where the road seems to dip and go back up, part of it goes straight, the other turns right. Guess what, since you've been running parallel with the tracks on your right for a while, you're going to turn right and run into Gates #3 & 4 the TWIN GATES. Be careful of the curve coming out of Gate #4 it turns sharply to the right. When you turned right you got onto Longhi Road.
4. Keep going "straight" on this road. Longhi Road will run into and you will get back on Lebanon Road. Keep following Lebanon Road past Heck Road, Bohnenstiehl Road, & Pense Acres. Shortly after Pense Acres turn left onto south Liberty Road. Follow this for a while and you'll go through Gate #5.

5. Just after Gate #5 S. Liberty Road will run into W. Mill Creek Road. Take that to the right. Gate #6 will appear briefly afterward.

6. Keep following W. Mill Creek Road over Scott-Troy/Troy-O'Fallon Road where it becomes E. Mill Creek Road. Watch for Blackjack Road and take it to the left. Look next for Bauer Road and take it to the right. Follow Bauer Road and it will take you to Gate #7.

7. Watch it…. Just after Gate #7 Bauer road comes out onto Hwy 40 and now nearly into Troy, Illinois.

Country Club Hills 60478

I-57 & Flossmoor Road
Murder sites are notoriously haunted because of the violence and tragedy that often takes place at these locations. The lonely stretch of Interstate 57 near Flossmoor Road was that much more rural back on June

3, 1973 when Henry Brisbon lured victims, Dorothy Cerny and James Schmidt, both 25, to their deaths by bumping their car from behind. When Cerny and Schmidt got out checking for damage, Brisbon accosted them. According to trial testimony, the couple pleaded for their lives saying that they were to be married in six months. However Brisbon told them, "Kiss your last kiss," then shot each in the back with a 12-gauge shotgun.

The scene of the Cerny-Schmidt murders has forever been scarred by this incident. The bodies were not immediately discovered but about ten years after the murders reports of a couple frantically trying to flag down cars at this area began to circulate.

One couple driving down the road had this happen to them. They were headed down I-57 back towards Chicago when they saw a couple on the side of the road trying to flag them down. This couple was aware of what had happened there previously and just did not have the guts to stop. They proceeded on until they found some police and described what had happened. The police officers drove back to find nothing out of the ordinary.

Others have had even a more frightening and puzzling scenario that transpires. Upon seeing a young couple needing assistance, witnesses have pulled their car on the shoulder and opened their doors to find no one along the expressway. In that short space of time, the ghosts have vanished.

Occasional reports still haunt the area and even though it's much more developed and urban then it was back in 1973, motorists keep a watchful eye to the shoulder of the road as they pass by Flossmoor Road. Especially those who remember the tragedy that took place here.

Crab Orchard Lake 62918

Route 13

In 1936 work was started on the Crab Orchard Creek Project. The purpose of this project was to construct three lakes for recreational use and as an industrial water supply. To make way for proposed lake a portion of Illinois Route 13 between Marion and Carbondale had to be relocated about a half mile to the north. Crab Orchard Lake was completed in 1939 by the Works Progress Administration (WPA). There are portions of Old Route 13 that still lie beneath the waters of Crab Orchard Lake. During times of extreme drought boaters can catch a glimpse of the old road.

Several night-time boaters have reported sightings of ghostly lights under the water in the vicinity of where the old road lies. Could these lights that are seen be the phantom cars of the 1920s and 30s that used to travel the old route?

Route 13 is also haunted by the ghost of a woman murdered along the highway years ago. You can hear her screams on occasion from the woods south of the highway near Crab Orchard Lake.

Crab Orchard Lake is located about four miles east of Carbondale, Illinois starting at Route 13 and Spillway Road and extends four miles past that intersection to Old Route 13 and County Road 10 (S. Division St., Carterville, IL). Some portions of Old Route 13 still exist, while other parts of it lie under the waters of Crab Orchard Lake.

Old Rt. 13 and Spillway Rd. (Carbondale, IL) is located at:
N37 deg. 44.3062
W89 deg. 8.8387

Old Rt. 13 and County Rd. 10 (South Division St. Carterville, IL) is located at:
N32 deg 44.2719
W89 deg. 4.6402

(Credit: Bruce Cline, director: Little Egypt Ghost Society)

East Dundee 60118

Duncan Avenue

Apparitions have been reported by people traveling on Duncan Avenue near the Fox River. These apparitions were reported by Horacio Minjares, a Carpentersville tradesman and civic booster, who heard them from his daughters and friends. His report is as follows:

"They are on Duncan near the bike path footbridge (under I-90). They are ghostly apparitions but very clear. At first you think that they are people because they appear to be solid, but when you look at them again, you realize there is a lack of color.

"The experience lasts for about four seconds. At the end of the experience they (witnesses) have to stop and throw up because of the intense emotional experience. Mostly it's been young people who have told me about it. I was skeptical but when my daughters saw them, I thought otherwise. They said they saw a woman in a lime green dress on, and although there usually is a lack of color, sometimes there is maybe a suggestion of color.

"This woman had a lime dress on, and they also described a feeling of intense sorrow and loneliness, but no fear. The apparitions are by the side of the road and in the woods there. I've heard numbers ranging from seven to eight people and up to 40 and 50 at one time.

"I first heard about it in November. Then I heard another story in the middle of December, and the girls experienced something in the first week of January. This usually happens before midnight. Two other sets of young people, a boy and girl and two brothers, between 17 and 22, also reported them.

"The first thing I asked them was, 'What were you smoking and what's going on?' But my middle daughter, Itzel, is an unbeliever and tends to have a rationalist attitude where everything has to be explained logically, and she was completely taken aback. So I thought maybe there's something to this.

"The lady in green was short, 5 feet tall, short dark wavy hair, she looks Latina. They were driving by when they saw this. They said they experienced a strange feeling and then there were people on both sides."

Itzel herself described the apparition as strange, but not scary.

"At first I wasn't sure what it was, but it gave me bad feeling and I knew it was something bad," said Itzel. "There were a lot of people. It was weird. It wasn't scary. I was with my older sister and she wanted to go back, but I wouldn't go back. The lady was standing on the east side of the road.

"It was very sad. The people we saw didn't look scary. They looked sad. That's what we both felt. We both felt really sick. I couldn't even talk. We felt sick like we wanted to throw up. We used to travel on that road often, but not anymore."

There doesn't seem to be any history to explain these strange occurrences at present. The GRS investigated this location on June 15, 1999.

(Credit: George Houde: Copley Press)

Elmhurst 60126

Lake Street & Frontage Road

The off ramp to North Avenue from the Tri-State Expressway (I-294) has been the site of another phantom hitchhiker. It is at this off ramp that a number of motorists have sited a most unusual hitchhiking character that also disappears.

He is seen as very pale, almost clown-like with having a bushy Afro similar to that sported by Art Garfunkel. He is always wearing sunglasses even in the evening and is often seen with big red lips, which would seem to be of a clown-type variety. The figure is dressed in an odd type of clothing and a white coat that has been described as bunny fur or perhaps a white-type raincoat.

He has been observed here on more than one occasion and it is surely a strange place to haunt unless he is coming from nearby Arlington Cemetery. Nearby, Arlington Cemetery was established in 1901 and which has some unusual fraternal markers such as the Bartenders or Waiters' along the southeast wall and a very complete Spanish-American Veteran's section.

There is absolutely no place for a figure to disappear in the area as there are no trees, bushes or other types of flora that could conceal an individual. Add to the fact that it's illegal in Illinois to be either hitchhiking or walking along an interstate unless your car has broken down. There is never any car seen in the immediate vicinity and by the time a passing motorist has a chance to slow down in order to assist this strange figure, he has vanished into nothingness.

Hickory Hills 60457

95th & Kean Avenue

The intersection of 95th Street and Kean Avenue is located at the edge of the Cook County Forest Preserves. Horse stables and riding trails were abundant in the area at one time and many used to partake of the lush flora and deep calming effect of the forest for horseback riding. However a number of riders and horses have been killed and injured attempting to cross the busy 95th Street that divides the riding trails. Vehicles traveling eastbound from La Grange Road often struck those who have attempted to cross. As the cars approach this intersection, they climb a small rise that obliterates equestrians and riders alike. When the horseback riders are finally seen, it is often too late. Several people were killed and some animals had to be destroyed due to the accidents.

At that intersection, some very unusual ghostly occurrences have been reported. There have been many reports of ghostly animals and riders attempting to cross the intersection after dark; long after the nearby horse stables have closed. One occasion, a husband and wife were traveling eastbound on 95th Street approaching Kean Avenue when they saw a semi-transparent figure of a horse and his rider crossing from north to south. As they came to the top of the hill, suddenly there was no one there! Both had apparently vanished into thin air.

The GRS investigated this location in November of 1982.

Werewolf Run

A small little-known cemetery right on the edge of the Cook County Forest Preserve district has been the site of local legends and alleged phantom animals for years. One urban legend tells of a tragic car crash in the 1950s in which the husband and wife were killed on the spot; however the baby was thrown from the vehicle and somehow survived. The child was never found, but instead of dying from the cold, the elements and lack of food, apparently thrived and, according to the legend, was raised by the wildlife.

The baby grew a thick coat of gray hair and lived just on the very edge of the encroaching civilization. Motorists would occasionally catch a glimpse of this creature in their headlights as they traveled through the area in the evening. However, history tells us that no such accident ever occurred there but the stories persist.

In the late 1970s a suburban housewife had a frightening encounter when a manlike creature bounded out of the neighboring woods directly into the path of her truck. She nearly hit the creature dead-on but instead it only glanced off the mirror, ripping it from its hinges. She thought about stopping incase she had hit an animal like a deer but decided against it due to the late hour and lack of physical evidence of a possible fatality. She brought her husband back to the accident scene the next day to search for her mirror and found it broken with spatters of blood nearby and embedded in the fragments of the mirror were swatches of thick brown fur!

A local avid horseback rider experienced something that still gives her the goose bumps even today. She was riding in the vicinity of Sacred Heart Cemetery in the summer of 1986 during a weekday, so the trails were virtually empty at the time. She decided to go down a smaller trail that is rarely used until her regular mare began to get highly agitated over something. She decided to take the animal back to the stables where it took quite a time in quieting down the horse.

Another rider had a similar experience in almost the exact same area when they heard a horrible commotion in some nearby bushes. It was as though someone or something was violently shaking the bush with an extreme amount of force. Suddenly as they approached the suspect bushes, the movement abruptly stopped. A thorough search of the bushes and immediate area revealed nothing that could have caused this incident.

However, passing motorists still describe seeing phantom animals that appear and disappear in the high-beams as they travel along Kean Avenue. These animals could be real wild animals except that they suddenly appear in the middle of the road rather than running from one side or another and disappear with moving to the left or right of approaching vehicles.

Justice 60458

Archer Avenue

Archer Avenue is by far the most haunted road in the Chicagoland area. Originally an old Indian trail, it was paved over in 1836 to make facilitate the construction crews and workers who were working on the Illinois-Michigan Canal which was completed in 1848. There are more haunted locations along Archer Avenue than any other road, street or avenue anywhere. The most famous is the hitchhiking ghost Resurrection Mary.

The legend of Resurrection Mary begins in the mid-1930s when a Polish-American girl went to a dance at the O'Henry Ballroom, named for the O'Henry Candy Bar. Today the location is known as the Willowbrook Ballroom. She apparently got into an argument with her boyfriend and began hitchhiking towards the Bridgeport area of Chicago along Archer Avenue when she was allegedly killed by a hit and run motorist.

Soon after this people began seeing an image of a girl in a long white ballroom gown and long blonde hair walking along the roadway looking for ride home. There have been thousands of similar reports and some have even claimed that she got into their car or cab before disappearing somewhere near the main gates of Resurrection Cemetery.

Near the entrance to the forest preserve and close to Fairmont Hills Cemetery, for quite a number of years there were consistent reports of motorists seeing a white to orange ball of light about the size of a soccer ball floating in the distance. As they approached the light, it suddenly would disappear but then reappear in their rearview mirror once they passed that spot. The light is no longer visible here but similar reports of a red light now frequent nearby Maple Lake.

Kean Avenue

A strange specter is seen is an old-fashioned, driverless hearse pulled by a team of mad horses foaming at their mouths. Sometimes seen along Archer Avenue between Resurrection and St. James Sag Church & Cemetery. Description of the hearse is a vehicle built from black oak and glass through which a small casket of a child can sometimes be seen. It has been linked occasionally to Resurrection Mary.

The hearse gallops at full speed towards Archer Woods Cemetery entrance but then continues down Kean Avenue before simply disappearing.

Why Not Drive-In

A ghost called Debbie driving her 1965 Ford Fairlane convertible allegedly haunts this small fast food establishment. Debbie is a ghost and loves to tell young men in the parking lot to follow her home and she'll go out with them.

On the way home, invariably she enters a fogbank or mist and disappears. Those who were following only her taillights as she enters the fog cannot seem to catch up to her as she out distances her pursuers. As they come out of the patchy fog there is no car and no taillights.

Debbie has allegedly given young men the slip on more than one occasion. At least one eyewitness gave a very detailed account of his encounter with Debbie and the Why Not Drive-In.

Lombard 60148

St. Charles & Grace

The ghost of a young boy haunts a dark section of St. Charles Road just before the intersection of Grace Avenue. The explanation of this particular haunting remains a mystery but speculation is that it could be that of a child who either was hit by a car while chasing something into the roadway or while walking along St. Charles Road late at night. An eyewitness describes his most terrifying experience.

"I was coming home one night at around 2 o'clock in the morning and I was heading down St. Charles Road and Grace. That's out in the western suburbs. I didn't have anything like this on my mind or anything and all of a sudden what appeared to me was a little boy crossing the road. He just stopped right in the middle of the road, right between the yellow lines. And then in slowing down, he wasn't moving or anything, so I just decided to go around him.

"It was about 2:30 or 3 o'clock in the morning. Instead of going around him, all of a sudden it wasn't a little boy anymore, it looked like something older running with my car and that kept up for about a half a minute and I guess my car was going about 35 to 45 miles an hour. When I turned back to look, it was still a little boy in the middle of the road just sitting there."

This interview was reported live on June 26, 1985 while this author was a guest on the cable show *Lifestyles* on Continental Cablevision. Later that same show, another caller related a similar encounter of a young boy he described as looking around five or six-years-old and appearing very white even though it was around 12:30 a.m. He thought it was a real boy getting ready to cross the street and he slowed down to avoid hitting him.

Directly across the street from where most of the encounters have taken place is a playground so perhaps the theory regarding a child playing nearby before being struck by a passing car might be a credible one.

Midlothian 60445

Bachelor's Grove Road

Bachelor's Grove Road is the trail leading into the most haunted cemetery that I have ever investigated to date, Bachelor's Grove Cemetery near Midlothian, Illinois across the street from Rubio Woods Forest Preserve along 143rd Street between Ridgeland and Central Avenues. The original road was the main thoroughfare before the Midlothian Turnpike was laid and then Bachelor's Grove Road was closed to vehicular traffic.

Up until the late 1970s you used to be able to drive down the road, turn around and drive out. Later they chained off the area and eventually raised the curb making that impossible except for Forest Rangers.

It is along this trail that goes for approximately ¼ of a mile that inexplicable encounters have been experienced including a phantom dog often described as a Rottweiler that looks very menacing sort of guarding the entrance to the trail. He is very quiet however and doesn't bark, growl or snarl and often disappears in the wink of an eye. Research Assistant Jim Graczyk of the GRS actually had a personal encounter there with several other eye witnesses.

A red skyrocket effect is seen whizzing up and down the trail very quickly and looks like a Roman candle.

The famous "phantom house" has often been encountered just off the trail by numerous people in the past and is always described in the same fashions; a white house, with white wooden pillars, a porch swing and a light burning dimly in one window. However if you leave the trail to try to enter or approach the house, it will shrink, getting smaller and smaller, until it simply vanishes from sight!

Ted Visnec and friends saw a deep blue light from the beginning of the trail back in the 1970s while visiting the location with friends. He was later literally pushed to the ground by unseen hands!

Millstadt 62260

Hernando's Bridge

Allegedly a man named Hernando hung his entire family over this bridge and then hung himself too. If you visit the site at night you can sometimes see the bodies still hanging over the bridge.

To get to Hernando's from Dupo; take IMBS Station Road off of Old Route 3 till you get to the little white church on the bluffs. Make a right onto Triple Lakes Road and take it all the way to Triple Lakes Golf Course. The old Lutheran Cemetery will be on the left. Make a right past the golf course. Take that road about two miles until the road comes to a T. Make a right and after about a half a mile, you will go down a hill. The bridge is at the bottom of the hill.

These stories are the same as told at Zingg Road except that this road is a little bit further to the east of the bridge between Millstadt and Belleville off State Route 183.

There is an added bonus of a house that you drive by that suddenly a ghost truck will come out and chase you. Both locations mention the Witch House which recent forums seem to indicate was torn down and isn't there anymore.

Palatine 60067

Palatine & Ela Roads

Hitchhiking ghosts have been a staple of American folklore for many generations. The hitchhiking ghost is most often female, usually called Mary and is often encountered on rural, deserted roads late at night. The ghost usually appears to be a flesh and blood person who is desperately in need of a lift or, at times, appears to be hitchhiking. Males tend to be the recipients of these spiritual wanderers and while conversation is usually limited to a few phrases, their disappearance is even more startling. Without the doors of the automobile being opened, the phantom is gone in a wink of an eye!

A male hitchhiking ghost has made his appearance known for many years along Palatine Road near the crossroad, Ela. This type of hitchhiker is better known in New York state and California rather then the Midwest. He's often been called the "Hitchhiking Jesus" because that's just how he appears to motorists.

Although he's not seen in robes as similar reports particularly around Buffalo, New York, this figure is dressed in very pale Levi-style clothing with long brown hair and a full beard. Very reminiscent of the 1960's hippie look.

Most people who encounter him particularly those who don't stop, look in their rearview mirror when they pass him only to see that he was no longer there, or upon stopping wasn't there either. He has been offered a lift several times by some brave souls who would pick up anyone anywhere no matter what the hitchhiker looked like. After he had entered the back seat, he is said to give a religious message, such as the end of world is coming soon or sinner repent and then disappears from the car!

Usually it's a very quick and frightening message and then it's all over. A remote possibility for this apparition lies in a small abandoned family-owned cemetery in a little field just southwest of that intersection. There are just a few graves, some without names and dates that have worn away. Is the hitcher a resident of that cemetery or an accident victim still trying to get home? No one knows for sure!

Palos Park 60464

123rd & La Grange Road

I personally interviewed a woman from the Denny's Restaurant at Southwest Hwy & Cicero Ave. in Oak Lawn named Dee on March 19, 1984 and she said how she and her boyfriend were traveling northbound on La Grange Road around midnight in January of 1984. They stopped at the light at 123rd and then both saw a misty cloud-like figure glide out of the woods towards the restaurant (Hackney's) from west to east and then just dissolve. Other people were also waiting for the light. I did not have the opportunity for any other corroborating witness accounts. They had not been drinking at all.

Nearest cemetery is located at 123rd and Will-Cook Road. This spot is very close to Horsetail Slough and Cap Sauer's Holding. On March 22, 1981 a girl's body was found dumped near Horsetail Slough near 123rd and 104th Avenue in Palos Hills. She had been stabbed and was only 15 years old.

Could this be the ghost of this untimely death trying to reach out from beyond the grave? Perhaps her last thoughts and aspirations were to try to get help and this was the nearest business or civilization sort to speak at the edge of the Cook County Forest Preserve.

St. Charles 60174

Munger Road

Allegedly was an old insane asylum on Munger Road that was haunted but it is now gone, if there were ever one to begin with. The train tracks seem to be the big draw now especially ever since 2011 movie came out.

Legends abound of a school bus full of children that stalled on the train tracks. A train coming full speed could not stop in time and the bus could get started again; the result was a tragedy. All the children were killed.

Since that unfortunate accident people have been visiting the site and claim if you stop your car on the train tracks, turn off the engine and put the car in neutral, the spirits of the children will appear and push the car off the tracks in order to avoid anymore loss of life. It is also said that if you sprinkle baby powder on the bumper and trunk of the car, you will see the little handprints appear, proof that there was some supernatural intervention here.

However no such accident ever occurred and Bartlett and other local police have had their hands full chasing away teenagers trying that because it can be dangerous.

Steger 60475

Axeman's Bridge

Located just off Old Post Road in south suburban Crete, Illinois is the remnants of an old rusted steel bridge spanning a small creek of running water. According to local legend an old recluse once owned that forested property did not take kindly to guests or trespassers. One evening two young teenagers invaded his property and crossed the bridge on a dare from others.

He allegedly caught the two on his property and before they had a chance to escape, he killed them both with a heavy ax he was carrying at the time.

Since that time, the bridge has fallen into a sad state of disrepair and is not safe to cross. In the woods, late at night, people have reported the figure of a man, wielding an ax that is said to be chasing a couple. Others claimed to have encountered the figure just as they cross what has been called Axeman's Bridge. However, the stories cannot be traced to any specific true happening in the past.

The GRS visited this site on October 28, 1993.

Steger Road & Western Avenue

Turning east on Steger Road from Western Avenue, one encounters a very rural, dark and forested road without any streetlights until one finally enters a residential area. It's along this dark stretch of roadway near the cemetery entrance, which has been the scene of multiple visitations of a small boy seen, riding a bicycle in the late evening or early morning hours. At least that's what it appears to be!

Motorists have almost ended up in collisions and accidents trying desperately to avoid hitting this young boy that appears out of nowhere and leisurely rides his bike across the two lanes of traffic without the slightest notion of impending disaster. Some cars have even spun around after hard braking. When they get out of their car to give him a piece of their mind, there's no one around and no place for anyone to have vanished that quickly.

Perhaps he is the unfortunate victim of an accident and is simply replaying the events leading up to his untimely death oblivious to the physical world!

Watseka 60970

Red Lantern Road

This location was investigated by the GRS on June 1, 1991 however we did not see anything unusual but did see a lot of car headlights. We were joined by the Kankakee Journal and some locals.

The story dates back to the 19th century and concerns a missing husband. The wife goes out searching for her husband with a lantern and the two of them are never seen alive again.

An amber to red light is sometimes seen down 1200N. It does appear to get closer before suddenly disappearing completely. Some say it is seen near a stone mailbox with no back and when you reach your arm inside, you will never find the other end. Of course this isn't true.

Directions:

1. Starting from Watseka, turn left (South) on S. Second Street.
2. Follow this road out of town, all the way to Woodland. Body Cemetery will be on the right.
3. Take a right turn (West) at the cemetery, then immediately take a left turn (South) on 1980E for 2.1 miles.
4. The road will curve twice, and after the second curve, turn right (West) onto 1200N. This is Lantern's Lane.
5. The site of the demolished house is 2.4 miles west, and the mailbox is 2.5 miles west.

INDIANA

Avon 46123

White Lick Creek Bridge

The legend of Avon's Haunted Bridge has been around for generations. Different rumors abound, but in general, the people of Avon have agreed that if you go near the old bridge at night, you will hear a moaning, discontented ghost, or maybe two or three of them. And if you cross the bridge on a hot summer day, you may see the ghost's tears on it.

There are various explanations for the hauntings. No one, of course, knows whether they are being carried out by a single ghost or many. Over the years, some theories have come to be popular regarding who the ghosts might be. A few of the most widely accepted versions are summarized below.

Henry Johnson, an alcoholic construction worker, slipped one night during the building of the bridge and fell into some wet cement, dying there in the lonely night. The following morning he was found, face frozen in the cement that killed him.

There is a similar report that an Irish or black construction worker fell to his death during the making of the bridge. He landed inside the framework of one of the bridge's supports. The railroad decided that, since the unfortunate laborer was already dead, they would simply inter his body in the bridge when they sealed the support with cement. Some say that the poor man's arm hung out, and they cut it off.

Perhaps, as some Avon residents aver, the ghosts on the Haunted Bridge belong to a young woman and her baby. The story goes that she was walking to the doctor's house late one night with her sick baby when she had the bad luck to get her foot caught among the railroad ties on the bridge. Then, disaster struck in the form of a huge locomotive barreling down on them. She struggled mightily, finally getting free of the railroad ties, but had no time to run across the bridge to escape the train. So, clutching her sick child, she jumped off the bridge. She survived, but the baby, falling from her arms, did not. Within a few weeks, the mother died of grief and a broken heart. The story concludes that if you drive under the bridge at night, you might very well hear her screaming for her baby.

The haunted bridge in Avon is still a functional railroad crossing, servicing the CSX Railroad, and regularly visited by residents and guests to get spine-tingling adrenaline rush. The GRS investigated this bridge on August 14, 2011.

Boonville 46071

Elizaville Road

Elizaville Road in Boonville is haunted. People report seeing a large seven foot tall man or a creature that looks like a man. The stories have been around since 1924, with locals claiming the man is obviously looking for something. Legend also claims that the man is responsible for the deaths and disappearances of dozens of people over the years.

Supposedly the best time to see this creature is between 1-3:30am.

Bremen 46506

Troll Bridge

Located just beyond Little Egypt Cemetery along Hawthorne according to some. According to others, the Troll Bridge was in a different location and it was torn down some time ago. This bridge is off of Hwy 331 on 5th Rd. going west.
It is a heavily patrolled location. Get permission to visit the bridge if you're going to be out here a night as you will be asked to leave (or fined, or worse) if you're caught loitering.

According to the Bremen police officer legend says that a group of teenagers had a car accident on the bridge, however, according to the police officer; this story was not likely to be true.

The Bridge is located along a dirt road in Amish country. The Bridge passes over a little creek near Lake of the Woods. There is a great deal of graffiti on the bridge unfortunately.

Disembodied screaming sounds are said to manifests here due to the car accident said to have occurred at the bridge. Also, reports of a tall shadowy apparition that will "throw things at you" have been reported.

Chesterton 46304

Route 6 Bridge

The location of this bridge is approximately two miles east of Highway 49 in Chesterton, Indiana. The legend goes like this; somewhere back in the early 1900s were manning the caboose at the end of the train. Supposedly as the train went through an underpass one of the men was momentarily distracted by something and when he looked for his partner, he was gone! Nobody seems to know what happened to him.

Some say he was pushed, while others suggest he fell or simply jumped from the train for some reason. To this day, people claim to see a figure of a man near that bridge; thought to be the man who is still trying to find the train and get back on.

Directions: It's any easy spot to find, but hard to find somewhere to park. Start by going down Hwy. 49, get off at the Rt. 6 exit and go east. Go about two miles and you will go up and over a bridge. This is the Route 6 Bridge.

There isn't really anywhere to park on the side of Route 6, so you might continue until you come to a side road called Mander Rd. After you come up to the tracks going down Mander Rd. there really isn't anywhere to park there either, but at least it's not as busy as Route 6. This might be as good a place as any to park and walk back to the bridge.

Columbus 47021

Haunted Bridge

This legend is similar to some of the Cry Baby Bridge stories but with a different twist. In this case, supposedly back in the 1920s, a woman had a child out of wedlock and apparently couldn't deal with all the finger-pointing and accusations of not having a husband so one evening becoming very despondent, she threw herself and her child off the middle of the bridge in an act of double suicide. The body of the woman was found however the baby never was.

Years later people that travel or visit the bridge around midnight claim to see a strange creature standing on two legs with piercing yellow eyes that is allegedly guarding the bridge. Those that are very close to the actual bridge have heard a baby crying.

On nights when a full moon is present, some say that you can actually hear the ghost of the woman calling for her child.

From Interstate 65 North take Exit 68 for IN-46 toward Nashville/Bloomington/Columbus. Keep right at the fork follow signs for Columbus and merge into IN-46/W Jonathan Moore Pike. Take a slight left at Brown St/IN-11 N/IN-46 E, follow that until you see Jackson St. on your left and turn into it. Keep going down Jackson and be sure to stay on the right once the road starts to split. Jackson should turn into Lawton St, and then take a left onto 11th St which you follow into a park. Once you arrive in the park drive your vehicle to the section of the parking lot in the back right near the woods. From here you continue on foot, you should be able to find the concrete path that leads into the woods. You don't stay on the path too long; you should be able to see the rocky embankment that you climb to the tracks directly on the path. Once you climb the embankment and reach the tracks at the top precede to the right and you should hit the bridge. WARNING: some parts of the bridge seem a bit unstable.

Ft. Wayne

Bostick Bridge

Bostick Bridge is a truss bridge that spans the St. Mary's River and is situated along Bostick Road. It was built in 1894 by the Canton Bridge Company and closed in April of 2004. The bridge is actually located on US Hwy 27 just beyond the I-469 overpass at Exit 11. Take Exit 11 to the right (Bostick Road) and follow it to the bridge.

Some of the reports include dead and mutilated animals nearby to the bridge and the intense feeling of being watched. The area is extremely dark at night, lacks streetlights and perhaps isn't the safest of places to be, especially if you are alone. When actually on the bridge, people have experienced knocking sounds and the bridge shaking for no apparent reason. More bizarre reports include bodies hanging from the bridge of a man and three children.

Francisville 47946

Moody Lane

A red or yellow, sometimes white, ball of light haunts a rural road just outside of Francisville, Indiana. Often called "The Moody Light" in respect to a local legend concerning a farmer called Moody who either was killed by chasing the killers of his daughter or by continuing to search for his daughter's body with a lantern on the night of her disappearance. You can take your pick, as there's nothing in the past history vaguely resembling this story.

The light is again seen at a distance and never close up. There's a long rural road stretching ahead of the viewer for a couple of miles. Locals say there's a tree or tree stump that marks the sight where the disaster happened long ago. If you wait silently in your car and face it down the long rural road and flash your lights on and off three times in succession, the light will suddenly appear and move closer to you.

The GRS has investigated this location twice in the past. The last time with researchers Stan Suho of the Ghost Research Society and Gary Hart on July 11, 1998. By using county maps and two separate sets of directions for finding the exact spot, we were able to finally pinpoint the correct viewing location. It was just a matter of waiting until dark and it wasn't long before we were seeing some lights at the end of the road that appeared to be getting closer before mysteriously vanishing instantly with apparently no where for them to disappear to!

After we viewed a few more of these sightings, with high-powered binoculars and spotting scopes, it soon became apparent that there were definitely car headlights approaching on a parallel road before turning off onto a road that was perpendicular and slightly below our visible horizon. The lights quite nicely diffused into two distinct automobile headlights. We had solved the mystery, much to the chagrin of some area locals who were curious as to what all the equipment was and what we were doing.

Again, locals don't often enjoy having their local legends squashed by skeptics, debunkers or serious researchers looking for logical explainable answers.

To find this location one must travel I-294 from Chicago, I-65 south to Rt. 30 east, 421 south to Francisville.

Greencastle 46135

Edna Collins Bridge

The Edna Collins Covered Bridge is located in Putnam County on County Road 450N and spans Little Walnut Creek. It was built in 1922 by Charles Hendrix and is a covered Burr arch-truss bridge. It can be found here: +39.72750, -86.97633. The GRS investigated this location on August 9, 2008.

The Edna Collins Covered Bridge is "generally" considered haunted ... it is said that sometime in the early 1920's a little girl would swim in the stream, which the bridge crosses. At the end of the day her parent would drive into the covered bridge, turn off the motor, and honk three times telling the little girl it was time to leave. One day the something had happened to the little girl causing her to drown. They say that if at night you drive into the bridge, turn off the motor, and honk three times the little girl will come and try to get in the car.

Griffith 46319

Reeder Road

Reeder Road is haunted by a woman named Elizabeth Wilson. During the 1950's a car veered off the road into the swamp and the woman drowned. Her body was buried in the nearby Ross Cemetery. The woman is sometimes seen walking along the side of the road and legend claims that if you pick her up, she'll disappear when you get to the cemetery.

There is a second version of the story and this one takes a different perspective on a classic urban legend tale. A couple was parked on the side of the road when they heard a noise outside. The boy went to investigate, and when he didn't return, the girl climbed out of the car to find him hanging from a tree above the car.

Many reports of various apparitions (figures in the woods, ghostly lights, voices, being chased by cars/ creatures). also, mostly due to the fact that it is surrounded by woods, various animal parts are frequently found along the road.

Directions: Take I-94 and get off on Cline Avenue South (exit #5). Take Cline Avenue for almost a mile and a half. Turn left onto US-6 also known as Ridge Road. Go a mile down Ridge road and turn right onto Colfax Street. Go just over two and a half miles and then turn left onto Reeder Road. Follow Reeder Road for about half a mile and you will come to a gate. That's were Reeder Road used to follow, but now it's just a dead end.

Lowell 46356

Indiana Bridge

There is a mansion a little bit further down the road that three people were apparently murdered and thrown off the bridge. Reports of cars rocking and thick fog appears out of nowhere. The GRS investigated this location on May 8, 2010.

Take I-65 to the Lowell exit and take a right on Clay St.

173rd & Holtz Road

When you are driving east on 173rd, there are two big hills. When you top either hill you can see the intersection of Holtz Road. When you top the first hill, occasionally you will see a bunch of flashing lights and what appears to have been a huge wreck. When the road continues, you lose sight of the intersection. When you see the intersection again, it is clear and there is no sign that anything was ever there. This has been seen by many people.

The GRS investigated this location on May 8, 2010 and did not see anything unusual.

(The Shadowlands Website: www.theshadowlands.net)

Michigan City 46360

Devil's Bridge

This is down a very dark dirt road in the middle of nowhere. Back in the 70's the police got word a few bodies were found buried here. They weren't really sure how they got here. They think it may have been a dumping ground for mafia hits that date back to the 20's or later. They think there are possibly many unfound bodies here. Psychics were brought out to try and find out about these deaths back in the 70's. They all refused to stay stating that the impressions there where very strong and painful.

Anyhow for years there have been signs of cult activity in this area, bonfires, strange happenings, animal sacrifices, etc. They had people messing around where these bodies had been. The state went so far as to fence off the underside of the bridge.

Location: Railroad Ave. and Ardendale Rd. in Pines, Indiana (it is like in Michigan City though, off of hwy 20)

Directions: From US 20 turn South on Ardendale Rd., right before the railroad tracks you will see a cement roadway (used to be dirt) to the east, turn east and up ahead you will see Devil's Bridge. 1750 E Railroad Ave, Michigan City, IN 46360

Mulberry 46058

Hamilton Road

According to Indiana folklore, this could be the most haunted road in Indiana, however a lot of people are unaware of the haunting or how to find this location. Take State Road 38 all the way to Mulberry and look for a road called 900 west. If you are coming from Lafayette, go right on it. You will come to a stop sign. Go thru the sign. That is Hamilton Road. There are three one lane bridges on this road, when you get to the third bridge, stop and flash your lights four times. As you then cross the bridge, you will see a short man in your rearview mirror chasing you.

Another fifty feet or so up the road will bring you to a graveyard. Park as close to the back of the cemetery as possible and walk along the fence. It is said that sometimes you can see flames coming from the woods. The flames allegedly mark the location where an old church burned to the ground in the 1800s killing everyone inside.

Just beyond the cemetery is a set of railroad tracks that is supposedly haunted as well. If you stop in the middle of the tracks around midnight, you will hear a train whistle and see lights coming towards you, and then the lights suddenly disappear. People claim to have sprinkled their bumpers with baby powder and later have found little fingerprints. Allegedly a boy named Danny was killed on the tracks in the early 1900s right after the tracks were built.

Portage 46368

Old Porter Road

Old Porter Road is haunted by strange creatures. There have been a number of tragic accidents on this stretch of road over the years, which some attribute to these odd figures. The creatures are described as looking like tall and skinny dogs with glowing yellow eyes. Even railroad workers claim to have seen these spectral animals running alongside their trains with glowing yellow eyes and howling loudly.

In the winter months late at night shadowy figures have been seen along the railroad tracks between Portage and Burns Harbor that run parallel with Old Porter Road. Nobody knows who these figures are or why they are haunting this location.

Travel to nearby Stagecoach Road where you can see figures in old fashioned clothing and strange lights in the sky.

Princeton 47670

Bulldog Bridge

Bulldog Bridge can be found east of town along the back roads of Princeton. Allegedly there have been many suicides attributed to the bridge most due to hanging however none have ever been confirmed through police or newspaper articles. There is also a story of a man found there on the bridge in his car with the doors locked and windows rolled up in the summertime and the temperatures were well into the 90s. He was decomposing quite badly already when he was found.

Some of the weird events reported there in the past include inexplicable cold spots even in the middle of the summer months where you can actually see your breath! This has been encountered by numerous people and investigators. A strange growling sound is sometimes heard in the nearby cornfields and perhaps this is where the bridge gets its name.

The area is heavily patrolled by police and game wardens so visit it at your own risk even during the daylight hours. Some have stated that the original bridge isn't there anymore but a replacement and the paranormal activity has completely ceased.

South Bend

Primrose Road

Directions: Take the toll road (80/90) east to exit number 72. Merge on to US-31 North. Take the Brick Rd/Cleveland Rd exit. Turn right on Brick Rd/Cleveland Rd. Brick Road will then go until a three way stop and you will be at Primrose Rd.

Local legend states if you drive your car along the road between 20-30 MPH your car will either stall or your tires will be mysteriously slashed. Cell phones die for no reason and if one walks down the road a bit they might encounter a phantom farmhouse. This is where some stories really get weird; a strange woman will sometimes appear and either grant you good or bad luck depending on how she feels about you.

Still further down the road, another farmhouse can be seen and horses galloping about and some claim to see the phantom horses running around. Allegedly satanic rituals were practiced out in the woods at night and you might catch a glimpse of ears peering through the trees at you! One such cult allegedly killed a young woman during a ritual one night and her ghost is said to haunt that section of woods and road.

IOWA

Boone

Kate Shelly High Bridge

This bridge is located approximately three miles west of Boone, Iowa and was designed by George S. Morrison for the Chicago and North Western Railway in 1901. It spans the Des Moines River with a length of 2, 685 feet and is 185 feet above the river itself. The bridge was renamed in 1912 in honor of Kate Shelly who saved a lot of people from immanent disaster.

On the afternoon of July 6, 1881, severe thunderstorms created a flash flood of Honey Creek that washed out the timbers of the trestle. A scouting party of four was sent out about 11pm to check on the condition of the bridge and they plunged into the creek. Hearing the crash Kate Shelly, knew there was an eastbound train due in within the hour and started across the span with only a lantern until it failed. Once across the span, she ran to the depot to sound the alarm and is credited with saving the lives of 200 people.

Reports of lantern lights on the bridge could be the ghost of Kate still reliving the events of that fateful evening. There have also been reports of phantom locomotives and a ghostly watchman.

Viola 52350

Matt's Bridge

The location of this bridge is unknown but could be associated with the Matsell Bridge Public Access area henceforth the name Matt's Bridge.

When cars are parked on the middle of the bridge, they are pushed across mysteriously. Others will hear and see "things" outside the car and sometimes handprints are seen on the bumper of pushed cars. Allegedly if you come back too many times, the ghosts will recognize you and will attempt to either push your car off the bridge or break the windows of your car! If you visit the location on a summer night and happen to have your windows rolled down, you might hear a lot of sounds and noises emanating from the nearby woods that sound very strange and unusual.

KANSAS

Barnes 66933

Coon Creek Bridge
The bridge is located about five miles south of Barnes on All American Road south of 5th Road spanning a creek.

People have observed an apparition of a young girl wandering through the woods on the east side of the bridge. There haven't been any reports of any deaths on the bridge or unusual accidents that would explain this presence. No sound ever accompanies her sightings and she is best seen just before sunrise.

Emporia 66801

Bird Bridge

Rocky Ford Bridge, known to locals as Bird Bridge is the bridge that Tom Bird (a minister) killed his wife, Sandy in 1983. It was at first thought to be an accident. Her car had gone over the side of the bridge and she was ejected. This stood for a short time, even with the proof of a struggle and questions as to why she would have been so far out of town in the first place.

Not long after Sandy was killed, Marty Anderson, husband of Lorna Anderson, was shot to death. Lorna pulled over to the side of the road (a country road) and told her husband there was something wrong with the car. He got out to investigate and was shot and killed by a masked man.

Anyway, it was found that Tom & Lorna were having an affair and planned to kill their spouses so they could be together. They were both sent to prison, although they are both out now. They made a movie based on the events, Murder Ordained starring JoBeth Williams and Keith Carradine in 1987.

If you are here late at night you might be able to here the screams of the woman and see an apparition walking to the shore down below. The bridge can be found on Round P and the Cottonwood River between Rt. 140 and 150 south of town.

Valley Center 67147

Theorosa's Bridge

Just about 12 miles north of Wichita, Kansas lay the small town of Valley Center, population a little over 5,000 people. Founded in 1872 along the Little Arkansas River, this town boasts a haunted bridge often known as Theorosa's Bridge at 109th and Meridian Streets. This bridge spans the Jester Creek at that point and is host to several tall legends.

One of the first stories told is from the 19th century and concerns some settlers that were attacked by a group of Indians. Their child, aptly named Theorosa was kidnapped and the couple set out in wagon train to an attempt to locate their child unsuccessfully. Their mournful cries in search for their child can still be heard today.

A second legend involves a skirmish between a cavalry and an Indian tribe living nearby. This time, an Indian woman is attacked, stabbed and her baby is thrown into the creek to drown.

A third tale concerns that a young lady named Theorosa had an illegitimate child and drowns the baby in the creek in order to hide her shame and guilt. Later, when the full scope of this deed finally sinks in, she drowns herself in the creek as well.

The bridge has been a hotspot of paranormal activity for many years according to locals. Eye witnesses have reported floating balls of lights, strange eerie shapes and the apparition of a woman that has been seen around the bridge. Cars seem to die out without any reason while driving or idling on the bridge itself, while other times the entire car appears to be shaking. Some have reported inexplicable cold spots from nowhere and the eerie cries of a child.

People report the weather at the bride is sometimes different from the surrounding area and if you call out to Theorosa and claim you have her child, she will come out of the water and attack you!

The original bridge burnt down in 1974 was rebuilt, destroyed again by fire in 1976 and then closed for the next fifteen years. Eventually in 1991, the road was reopened to vehicular traffic.

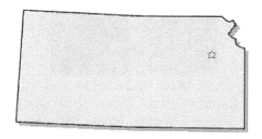

KENTUCKY

Corbin 40701

Florence Road

At the intersection of Florence Road and Early Addition Street, people have experienced what can best be described as a zone of fear or being watched even though no one is around. These unusual feelings dissipate once one leaves this area, only to return again if one enters into that intersection. There haven't been any accidents or tragedies that have occurred here that might explain why people feel this way.

This most often happens to pedestrians walking this area then to motorists as they move more slowly and are actually in the area longer than automobiles.

Garrard County

Camp Nelson Covered Bridge

Photo taken by James McCray

The original Camp Nelson Covered Bridge was built in 1838 by Lewis Wernwag and was a 240 feet double barreled covered bridge that Union troops actually used during the Civil War. It remained in use until 1926 until a truck fell through the floorboards.

A new bridge was built that same year but it too was eventually closed to traffic and demolished in 1933. All that remains of the original bridge are the stone approaches and a preserved façade on the northern approach. The bridge that replaced this bridge was also replaced by another one in 1972.

One can see the remains of these bridges just off Rt. 27 (Danville Road) on Camp Nelson Road and Old Danville Pike. +37.76974, -84.61718.

Harrodsburg 40330

Hank's Bridge

The local legend of Hank's Bridge was that Hank, a black man, was hanged in the 1940s under the bridge. Kentucky State Coordinator, Dave Guss, talked to a local couple that was at the campground. They live near the bridge and they said they never feared it.

The story goes if you stop on the bridge, your car will not start for awhile, and you will be pushed across. Dave indicated that nothing unusual happened to him during his visit.

The bridge spans Salt River and is located on Lower Salt River Road. Head south on S College St./KY-152/US-68 toward KY-152/Mooreland Ave/US-68. Turn right at KY-152/Mooreland Ave/US-68, turn left at Quirks Run Road, and continue on Lower Salt River Road. This will lead you right to Hank's Bridge.

Lexington 40507

Eyeball Bridge

A short drive out a county road called Russell Cave Road and Huffman Mill Pike in Lexington, Kentucky and you will find yourself sitting on top of what locals refer to as Eyeball Bridge. The local legend is that the bridge was part of an old wagon trail that settlers used to travel through the Kentucky countryside. One day a band of Indians scalped the women and removed their eyes and threw them into the creek. Of course, once the town's folk found out, a mob was formed. The mob sat and waited for the Indians to return and sprung their trap. The men took the Indians and cut their eyes out and hung them from the bridge to die a slow agonizing death as their eyeball's floated in the water looking up at them.

This bridge would become the site of many more murders and hangings and every time the person eye's were cut out and thrown into the water. After a period of time, people started noticing on full moon lit nights that if you looked into the water, the light would reflect just right and you could see what appeared to be eyes looking back up at you. Later in time this would become a local haunt and everyone would make fun and jokes of the place, until that is on a full moon lit night when they would look into the water, and see it looking back at them. Eventually someone painted a huge eyeball in the middle of the bridge and it was said that this was the only place you would be safe if those that had lost their eyes came back looking for them.

Paranormal activity in this area is strong and there are many things you can encounter, from woman and children screaming, Indian calls, and a woman in an old dress walking the bridge who disappears right before your eyes. I grew up going to this bridge and taking others as I got older and it has never let me down. So if you ever find yourself on a winding county road in Lexington, Kentucky and you happen to come up on a bridge with an eyeball painted on it. Be sure to stop in the center over the eyeball and roll your window's down and listen. Just remember, if it's a full moon out, get out and take a peak over the side if you dare.

(Credit & story by: Chris Dedman, paranormal investigator)

LOUISIANA

Broussard 70518

Mary Jane's Bridge

Many people believe that what is called Mary Jane's Bridge is actually Bayou Tortue Road Bridge which is located on Bayou Tortue Road. That road is continuous with Garber Road, intersecting with Highway 90 further north toward Broussard. Bayou Tortue Road eventually becomes Parish Road 140 a bit further south.

The story has been told for many years and concerns a girl that visits the bridge with her prom date. Allegedly he rapes and murders her, eventually throwing her lifeless body over the bridge. Her body was never found and no one was ever charged with the crime if the event really happened at all. This is the reason for all the apparitions and activity that have been reported throughout the years locals say.

There are rumors of satanic rituals that have taken place near the bridge in the past.

In August of 1985, a retired police officer had a bizarre encounter at the bridge that made a believer out of him. He felt a weird presence at the bridge that motivated him to get out of the car and explore the area a bit more. Upon exiting his vehicle, he observed a woman in white with long flowing brown hair. He asked her if she needed any help but there was no reply. She just stared back at him. He felt a distinct chill in the air at that time even though it was a warm summer evening. The apparition was apparently bathed in an eerie blue light!

New Orleans

Mona Lisa Drive

The City Park in the heart of New Orleans is quite large and encompasses some 8,000 acres. Near the turn of the 20th century a well-known philanthropist donated a number of statues. There were so many that New Orleans Parkway Commission didn't quite know what to do with all of them. One statue in particular however was to be given special treatment in accordance to the donor. The beautiful bronze gothic statue depicted his daughter Mona and was to commemorate her death. This statue was to stand alone.

The statue was placed along a mile long promenade to a cul de sac where it would be placed on a pedestal. Everyone loved the place chosen including the donor.

However as it was somewhat of a secluded spot, it eventually became a hangout for teenage lovers or even drinking parties. One evening a car chase through the park and around this statue resulted in one of the cars striking the pedestal and the statue of the Mona fell to the ground. The remnants of the broken statue were transported to New Orleans Museum of Art.

Not long after this accident that rumors and stories began to circulate about the ghost of Mona being seen near the site where the statue once stood. The ghost was described as a lady in white with a mournful or pained expression on her face. Reports would indicate that she would often float around the area and sometimes peer into the passenger side car windows of those who visited the site at night. This could be accompanied by the sound of her scratching on the car windows as well. Then after a very sad look on her face, she would fade into nothingness! Most of these reports seem to happen in the spring.

The location today is completely overgrown by vegetation and the road is unusable. It is not far away from Popp's Fountain and all that remains is the pedestal where that statue used to sit on top of buried in the weeds.

MAINE

Brunswick 04011

River Road

Along River Road are five mysterious stone markers; two are easy to find while three others require a bit of searching to locate them. Some stand six feet high or more and have markings on them. No one seems to know what they represent or who might have erected these markers. Locals believe that they could have been placed there by early settlers to mark their territories while others believe that Native American Indians are responsible for these stone structures.

Whoever built these monoliths may remain a mystery however people who visit the locations at night under a full moon claim various strange activities happen to them including the sounds of voices and singing.

Millinocket 04462

Brownville Road

The White Lady haunts Brownville Road and the Green Bridge. She can often be seen walking alongside the bridge late at night.

The legend of the ghost states that somewhere back in the 1940s a couple traveling in a car careened off the bridge but were uninjured. The husband told the wife to stay in the car while he went off to get some assistance. When he returned to the area, his wife was nowhere to be found. Since then her ghost is said to haunt this area where she disappeared.

Mysterious thick patches of fog will suddenly emerge and engulf you and your car should you happen to visit the bridge on occasion and you might just be lucky enough to catch a glimpse of the White Lady. Locals say that there is indeed a car fitting that era at the bottom of the ravine lying on its roof, so perhaps there is something to the story after all.

Rockport 04856

Goose River Bridge

During the Revolutionary War, the town of Rockport was known as Goose River and had an active role in the war. British soldiers often raided the town looking for food, guns and supplies to sustain themselves during the war against the colonies. There was also a lot a guerilla warfare and skirmishes, where small pockets of resistance fought against the British invasion. One man who took part in these raids was William Richardson.

Richardson even helped a man named Samuel Tucker in 1779 capture a British ship loaded with goods and supplies. He acted as the guide to bring the ship safely to port in Goose River. This pleased him that he had did his part in the war effort, however the British did eventually pillage and burn the town down before the war ended.

After the peace treaty was signed in 1783, the people of Goose River decided to celebrate by having a huge party. Richardson, of course, was the biggest partier that evening filling everyone's cup to overflowing and indulging a bit too much himself.

Later in the evening, Richardson wandered away from the party down the darkened streets of Goose River, pitcher of ale in hand when he came across three strangers. He offered them a drink but these strangers just happened to be Tories, or British sympathizers. One of them struck Richardson with the blunt of their rifle to his head and left him there on the bridge to die.

To this day, people have encountered a ghost locally known as "The Pitcher Man." This ghost is seen still trying to offer people a drink as they near the point where he died on the bridge. Some have reported seeing this apparition walking silently behind them while others have had Richardson thrust a pitcher through the opened windows of their cars as they drive over the bridge.

MARYLAND

Bowie 20716

Governor's Bridge

The get to Governor's Bridge from Washington, D.C., take Rt. 50 east toward Annapolis. Get off on 301 South (Crain Hwy.). Then, turn left onto Governor Bridge Rd., if you get to Patuxent River Rd., you've gone too far.

The story here concerns a woman who became pregnant out of wedlock and because she was ridiculed and ashamed when the child was born, she went to the bridge and threw the baby off the bridge into the river below. She soon became very depressed and decided to end her own life the same way and jumped from the bridge to her death.

A different version of the story is told about a family that ran off the bridge with their car and perished except for the baby that later died in the hospital. Visitors to the bridge at night have heard the sounds of a baby crying and disembodied screams.

Sometimes a visual apparition of a woman is seen standing in the middle of the bridge. This often frightens people and supposedly a truck driver a number of years ago swerved to avoid hitting the woman he saw standing on the bridge. Later when police come to the scene to investigate why a woman would be there in the middle of the night, they find no evidence that anyone was ever there.

Other reports claim that the woman is seen below the bridge in the water often soaking wet looking very confused and lost. Another weird phenomena people report when driving along Governor's Bridge Road towards the bridge is the dark shape of a car and headlights following them. The car speeds towards the rear bumper as though it's going to strike the car from behind before suddenly completely disappearing.

The GRS visited this location on August 10, 2009.

Hebron 21830

Hebron Spooklight Road

To reach this location travel down Highway 37 in Wicomico County in eastern Maryland, six miles northwest of Salisbury off US Hwy 50. The light was actually seen on the current Church Street.

The Maryland State Troopers had their hands full just before midnight on the clear but steamy night of July 16, 1952. Trooper Robert

W. Burkhardt and a sergeant were on routine patrol just a mile west of Hebron, Maryland and had just turned onto Church Street Extended, a mile-long stretch of road lined by trees on both sides. Off in the distance, a circular yellow ball of light was observed slightly above the road and moving toward the car.

"It's either an old car with one dim light or a wagon lantern that should be red," the sergeant was quoted as saying in *Mysterious Fire and Lights by Vincent Gaddis.*

Whatever it was began to rapidly close on the vehicle, moving directly in the middle of the road. At the last possible moment, to avoid a collision, the trooper swerved off the road unto the shoulder and skidded to a rather abrupt stop. According to the two troopers, the light suddenly stopped and hovered in the glare of their headlights approximately twenty feet away. As they restarted the car and began to approach the object, it receded. And as they gained speed toward the light, the object matched the squad's speed and kept the same distance. As the car reached a speed of forty miles per hour, the light inexplicably vanished!

Not wanting to risk ridicule, Burkhardt returned the following night with five other patrolmen and found the light was already there on Church Street waiting for them. They all exited their vehicles and attempted to surround the light, which abruptly winked out and then reappeared in a nearby field!

Several days afterwards, additional officers, including Edward H. Bracey, pursued the object for over a half-mile before the globe veered off the road at fifty miles per hour into a field.

"It was just like a neon tube when you turn it out," Burkhardt said. "It faded slowly into a reddish glow which finally went out."

Lieutenant C.C.Serman, commander of the State Police Barracks in nearby Salisbury was also counted among the many witnesses to this bizarre phenomenon during the summer of 1952. He described it as "about the size of a wash basin, usually at the height of an automobile headlight and about the same intensity."

Suddenly, it stopped as abruptly as it started even though older residents claimed it had been showing up periodically for half a century.

The *Salisbury Daily Times* featured a story, "Professor Believes Ghost Light is Gas," in which a John Hopkins professor alleged that gas was being generated by decaying vegetable matter seeping to the surface and being moved around by a gust of wind. The professor stated, "It seems a shame to have state police out there all night trying to catch a little bag of gas."

The sightings apparently, according to some eyewitnesses, continued to occur off and on until after the road was blacktopped. The Wicomico County Road Division records the road being tarred and chipped in 1953, widened and rebuilt in 1958, and blacktopped in 1974. It may have been that dust from the old, original dirt road was reflected in automobile headlights providing the "Ghost Light Road" illusion.

Another more far-fetched theory was offered that included a broken shard of glass being carried into a low-hanging branch by a possum or raccoon. As cars would approach, their headlights would reflect into the glass, but just to a point before disappearing.

Local legend provides some other paranormal explanations, including that years ago when the railroad was being built, a man with a lantern was killed there and the light is his lantern. There is also a tale of a gambling dispute that resulted in a murder in this wooded area and the ghost of the murdered gambler haunts the road.

Another legend states a black man was hung in the woods and left to die and it's his spirit that looks for the light of justice, and finally, a local man committed suicide by hanging himself in the nearby forest and his body was never found until many years later.

The GRS visited this site in November of 1988 with some friends from a local bulletin board service (BBS), when those used to be quite popular. The road, properly called Old Railroad Road runs exactly two miles from US Route 50 until it bends off sharply to the left and intersects Main Street. The sightings were most often encountered between Portermill Road exactly one mile south of Route 50 and Church Street Extended, which is another half-mile south.

I found it very interesting that even though the light had been inactive since the mid-1970s, a high-voltage power station was a quarter-mile further south of the actual sightings. While this may not mean anything, it might explain a lot.

Joppa 21085

Jericho Covered Bridge

The Jericho Covered Bridge can be found in Harford County at 39.4598298, -76.3874608. This is the only covered bridge in the county.

According to most websites, this bridge was built in the early 1800s and was the scene of many lynchings and hangings especially during and after the Civil War. I found the last part of that statement a little harder to verify especially since according the Jerusalem Mill Village website, they indicate that the current bridge dates to December of 1865 which would put it after the Civil War had ended.

Nevertheless, if you believe in the story, many were hung from the inside rafters and if you drive through the bridge at night and happen to glance in your rearview mirror, you might be shocked to see images of swinging bodies still hanging from the rafters.

MASSACHUSETTS

Lexington 02420

Battle Road

This was the location of "the shot heard round the world," the first confrontation between the British and militiamen in the town of Lexington on April 19, 1775. The British troops numbering nearly 700 strong under Lt. Col. Francis Smith had orders to disarm and destroy and munitions that they found on the "rebels." They were greeted by about 80 militiamen under the command of Captain John Parker. He placed his troops in plain view of the approaching redcoats, not hiding behind obstacles and not blocking the road to Concord.

A British officer road to the front of their ranks and ordered the militiamen to stand down and drop their weapons. Parker did later tell his troops to disperse and go home but before this could happen, the British opened fire on the militiamen, killing eight without any provocation. The Revolutionary War had begun!

Near the current day Captain Smith's house is where the first shots were fired. Allegedly British soldiers are buried along this trail. People have reported feeling fearful and frightened near the spot where this skirmish took place in the early morning hours at 4am. Others have seen apparitions of children near this spot as well.

Rehoboth 02769

Route 44

The route is famous for a colorful ghost; the redheaded hitchhiker of Route 44. This is by far the most famous ghosts in Massachusetts as it's been reported for several decades. This redheaded figure of a man is often seen hitchhiking for rides along Route 44, or is waiting to be picked up.

Other times he is simply seen walking in the middle of the road and some have even claim to have passed right through him. One bizarre report tells of seeing his face outside of a speeding car traveling at 40 miles per hour!

Nobody can be certain who this ghost is even though there have been accidents and fatalities there including a man who seems to slightly match the description of the ghost. People often describe him as being over six feet tall, very sturdily built with red hair and a full red beard to match. The clothes very but look like work pants or jeans with a red flannel shirt.

A typical encounter is where a man is viewed at the scene and someone stops to render aid or give him a lift. However as soon as they stop, the person is simply no longer there and has vanished only to be followed by some audible laughter or screaming.

Numerous reports of the apparition sometimes either appearing in the rearview mirror of the car or in a vacant seat has been reported in the past and can be quite unnerving. At times it is said he can interfere with the function of the car, making it stall or the radio quickly scanning through stations, sometimes with a demonic-sounding laughter heard through the car speakers.

MICHIGAN

Algoma Township

Hell's Bridge

This is popular urban legend and concerns an alleged child killer called Elias Friske back in the mid 1800s. He was a preacher that preached fire and brimstone. He eventually convinced the townsfolk that the devil had carried away some of their children so they organized a search party and off they went leaving the old, frail Elias to watch over their remaining children. Not soon after they left, Elias talked the children into walk towards the river after roping them together, saying that they couldn't afford to lose anymore children.

After awhile an intensely horrid odor was noticeable and became stronger and stronger; it was the dead and skinned bodies of the other missing children. One by one, Elias killed the other children and threw them into the river and ran away. After the townsfolk came back and found their children missing, they followed the tracks to the river and were horrified to find their murdered children. They were able to follow Elias' tracks and bring him back. He claimed the devil had entered his body and forced him to kill all those youngsters. The parents hung him from the bridge and later had the river carry his body away.

Today, the location is known for a lot of different paranormal activity including the feeling of hands grabbing ones feet from beneath the bridge, children laughing or screaming, disembodied footsteps, the sight of glowing eyes in the woods at night and a dark apparition standing on the bridge with red glowing eyes. A lot of these encounters seem to happen around the stroke of midnight.

Algonac 48001

Morrow Road

This is one of Michigan's oldest legends and ghost stories probably dating back to the late 1800s. The gist of the legend is about a woman haunting Morrow Road looking for her lost child.

The road is located in southeast Michigan and used to be a cattle trail before being converted into a dirt road for cars and trucks.

Allegedly a woman whose initials were I.C. died an untimely death along Morrow Road searching for her young boy. Because the passion was so great in life to find her child, she still continues to search for him even after death.

There are many, many legends or stories as to how she and the boy died. Some believe the boy was kidnapped but no ransom was ever announced and she died searching for him. In one case, the boy drowned because the mother wasn't watching him all the time. In this instance, the boy was indeed found, dead and the mother committed suicide by hanging herself.

Another story is that they lived in a two-story house that was broken into by burglars and they were both murdered by in the intruders.

Some believe that he was last seen alive near a fire and that eventually even the mother died in some kind of fire.

Another way that they died is that they both froze to death. The boy went outside in the cold; the mother went to search for the boy but also froze to death in the process.

A popular belief is that the boy was murdered by the bridge which led the mother to search there. The would-be murdered lying in wait raped and then killed her also.

An unpopular theory in the 1950s of something called the Morrow Road Monster killed the boy. This one is very farfetched.

But whatever story you believe, many have encountered something quite unusual or hearing the child on or near the road. The woman is always seen wearing a light blue nightgown, searching with bloody hands for her child. Frantic screams can sometimes be heard yelling, "Where's my child?"

If you stop along Morrow Road where the southern bridge used to be and honk your horn three times, sometimes you will hear a baby crying in the distance. People have been chased by multi-colored orbs of light which could be the spirits of those two.

Fallasburg 49331

Fallasburg Park Covered Bridge

Fallasburg Covered Bridge was built in 1871 by Jared N. Breese of Ada, Michigan. The cost of the bridge was only $1500 and it has been repaired in 1905, 1945 and 1994.

Local legend tells of a witch that was hung somewhere in this area in the 1800s, perhaps she is the same one called the "Ada Witch." Allegedly she rests in Findlay Cemetery. Also there is a story about a young man who committed suicide by drowning at this bridge.

Apparitions have been seen in the area as well as the sounds of voices.

Grosse Ile

Knock Knock Road

Actually known as Strasburg Road near the Detroit/Grosse Ile area, the road is scene of the apparition of a little girl often seen around two o'clock in the morning. Suddenly you might hear a knock on the driver's side window of your car and the little girl is there standing there. Apparently she is still looking for the person who killed her on the road so many years ago. Some say this story may date back as far as the 1940s.

Another story claims that a man and a woman went out along Strasburg Road to a well-know "lover's lane." Apparently he got disgusted because he was turned down by the woman that evening so he threw her out of his car and slammed the door. Supposedly the woman's hair or dress (depending on which story you believe) was caught in the door and he dragged her down the road to her death.

According the Detroit News from June 12, 1962, this story is absolutely true. The knocking that people often hear as they pass the location where the woman died is the ghost of the woman banging and knocking on the side of the car, trying to get the driver's attention to make him stop the car.

Sidnaw 49961

Perch River Bridge

Eye witnesses report an older 1930s sedan that comes down from the hill, paused momentarily before the bridge, stops and continues across the bridge and then disappears into thin air.

Perhaps in the 1920s or 1930s, a car was attempting to cross the bridge during the spring when the snow was melting. The river was very high and the bridge was completely washed out. Apparently the driver never saw this and drove off the bridge killing himself, his wife and his young daughter.

Watersmeet 49969

Route 45

Ghost lights are not only a mystery to behold but sometimes are noted tourist attractions and the "Mystery Light" between the towns of Watersmeet and Paulding in Michigan's Upper Peninsula is just that. The Watersmeet Business Directory flyer describes the light prominently on the back page:

"While in Watersmeet you should see 'The Mystery Light'.

"The 'Light' has defied explanation since it was first observed about a dozen years ago, although theories abound. To observe the phenomenon, one must drive north from Watersmeet on US 45 for four miles toward the neighboring village of Paulding, and take Robbins Lake Road for a short distance west – an unimproved rural lane once part of a military road authorized by Abraham Lincoln during the Civil War in anticipation of a British attack through Canada.

"By tramping through dense woods to the summit of nearby hills, the mysterious light can be observed almost every night once darkness has descended on the northern wilderness.

"It appears to rise slowly out of the forest and then hovers low in the sky for varying intervals – ranging from a couple of minutes to over a quarter of an hour. Often described as looking like a 'bright star' it first seems to be a campfire ember, reaching an intense reddish glow, then becoming a haze and finally receding to a mere spark before disappearing into the night.

"Explanations vary from fanciful to factual. Some say it's the spirit of a long dead mail carrier ambushed by Indians over a century ago; others insist it is the ghost of an engineer killed in a nearby railroad accident in years gone by. One woman thinks it's a mystical sign of religious significance.

"In the meantime, The Mystery Light, continues to baffle, intrigue and mystify the visitor."

According to locals, the light has been seen since around 1870. It has appeared in various local newspapers and many have made the trek out to the observation point to view and be mystified by this light for decades.

The Ghost Research Society decided to investigate this location for almost a week from September 13th through the 21st of 1986. We were joined by two former members of the GRS Richard Locke and Richard Kerscher, both of whom told me that they simply believed the lights were nothing more than car headlights and taillights seen in the distance. I still wanted to see for myself and prove or disprove the story.

We interviewed dozens of eyewitnesses, collected topographical maps of the area, talked to local forest rangers, drove Route 45 itself where the light is actually seen and viewed the like both from Robbins Pond Road and Dingman's Rock.

Through high-powered binoculars the lights defused quite nicely into a pair of automobile headlights but I still wasn't complete with the tests and experiments that I wanted to perform.

Next morning, we traveled north beyond the viewing point along US 45 toward Paulding. We located the small cemetery mentioned in the traveler's brochure and carefully plotted mileage from that point back to the observation points. We observed that the mileage is close to eleven miles as reported but perhaps less, since the point where the lights are first picked up are at the top of a large hill; elevation over 1,500 feet above sea level and nearly 200 feet higher than Maple Grove Cemetery. From that point, it's exactly 8.3 miles to Robbins Pond, which is also old Highway 45.

So what the observer is actually seeing are car lights topping the hill, occasionally dimming their high-beams for oncoming traffic, taillights of those oncoming cars passing the first cars, then their high-beams coming on again and then the cars finally disappearing into a deep slope in the road. By timing when the lights vanish from sight and when they pass behind you on US 45 at an average speed of 55 miles per hour, it calculates to approximately seven minutes!

Stopwatch tests were performed to calculate the average amount of time the lights were in view at an average speed of 55 miles per hour and found this to be 90.2 seconds. By recreating the driving experience from the crest of the hill at 55 miles per hour for 90 seconds, we were relatively sure of the exact point on US 45 where the mysterious lights vanish from view. From that point in the road, the observation point could no longer be seen.

During our last evening, we set up a video camera at the observation point and I had a driver come down the road from the crest of the hill with the four-way flashers on. He was also instructed to blink his high-beams on and off every five seconds. The results were conclusive! We recorded the oncoming vehicle on tape flashing the bright lights every five seconds on cue! We had proved, beyond the shadow of a doubt, that the lights that visitors have been seeing for over twenty years were simply headlights and taillights and the terrain of the area, which causes them to disappear in a mysterious manner. I was elated however, predictably, the locals did not agree with our results and findings.

MINNESOTA

Forest City 55389

Mystery Road 660

As one travels through Forest City, Minnesota on Road 330, it will eventually turn into Road 660. The road does appear to be perfectly level and some even bring levels just to prove that fact. Once arriving on that road, if you put your car in neutral and turn it around, it will be pulled backwards.

Many people believe there is some weird electromagnetic fields in play here due to visitors experiencing severe headaches which quickly dissipate upon leaving the area.

Minneapolis

Arcola Trail Bridge

The bridge can be found approximately twenty miles east of downtown St. Paul/ Minneapolis, Minnesota. To reach the actual location of the bridge, take MN-95 between Stillwater and Taylor Falls to find Arcola Trail. The road is not very long, approximately four miles and some parts are paved while other parts are gravel. The bridge is located along this road. It is nearly a mile long and spans the Saint Croix Valley between the village of Arcola, Minnesota and Somerset, Wisconsin.

The bridge was built by the Wisconsin Central Railroad and opened in 1884. This bridge was added to the National Register of Historical Places in 1977.

This bridge is known to locals as High Bridge and isn't in the greatest of conditions. Extreme caution should be used if you intend to actually walk on the bridge itself. There is a report of a couple that was looking for the ghost one evening on August 10, 2008 and the woman, 20, attempted to cross the bridge around 1am when a plank on the walkway gave out and she fell 200 feet to the ground. Rescue workers pronounced her dead at the scene. Her male companion was not injured.

The ghost of the Arcola Trail Bridge is that of White Lady that is supposedly in search of her lost husband. Another sighting is that of a blue ghost light seen near the bridge at night. Sometimes she is seen walking around with a lantern searching. Perhaps these are the spirits of unfortunate people that have perished out there in the past.

MISSISSIPPI

Columbus

Three-legged Lady Road

Its real name is Nash Road. Turn off of Hwy 45 onto Wilkins-Wise towards the lock and dam. Then turn left at the stop sign (if you turn right you'll go to Proffitt's Porch; if you go straight you get to the lock). It's an immediate right after that. The church is gone now. It's a gravel road that eventually runs into Plymouth Rd. Turn left onto Plymouth and it'll take you past the Sports Page and back to Hwy 45.

There are several local legends about the three-legged lady that is often seen as a ghost, running alongside your automobile and banging on the doors, often allegedly leaving behind dents in the metal.

One was that she lived on Nash Road and had an affair with a Civil War veteran. Her husband found out about this, killed him and dragged his body down the road dismembering his limb on the bridge. She later found the limb and stitched it on her own body as a remembrance of their love affair. She eventually went crazy, killed her husband, committed suicide and now haunts the church (not there anymore) and the road.

The second story is that she caught her husband cheating on her, killed him and cut him into little bits except his leg which she sewed on her body. She later buried the rest of him in the nearby cemetery.

The last, most disgusting rendition of this tale, involves a weird medical condition that the woman had where her organs had to be strung together and hung outside of her body. They resembled a human appendage of a leg.

Whatever story you believe, it surely would be it would be a most bizarre apparition to behold!

Meridian 39302

Stuckey's Bridge

Stuckey's Bridge spans the Chunky River just about twelve miles outside of Meridian, Mississippi. The original bridge was constructed around 1850 however a newer structure was commissioned by the Virginia Bridge and Iron Company in 1901. The bridge was placed on the National Register of Historic Locations on November 16, 1988.

According to local legend a member of the infamous Dalton Gang named Stuckey owned a nearby inn where he would rob and murder his clients and then bury their bodies near the riverbank of the bridge.

Allegedly after having murdered twenty people, Stuckey was finally apprehended and lynched from the side of the bridge. Not long afterward, rumors began to circulate of a ghost of a man seen around the location at night carrying a lantern and sometimes the sound of a loud splash which people say is that of Stuckey's body hitting the water after his lifeless body was finally cut down. Others report his deformed body still hanging from the side of the bridge during certain nights.

MISSOURI

Fetus 63028

Highway A
There is a haunted railroad crossing located along old Highway A, also called Hillsboro Road. From I-55 take Old Hwy A west for 1.9 miles to the railroad crossing marked on the map as Silica. This location is reported to be haunted after a fatal traffic accident occurred when an automobile was struck by a passing train. A ghostly couple haunts the railroad tracks and is sometimes seen holding hands.

(Credit: Route 66 Paranormal Alliance)

Jefferson City 65110

Old Highway 94
This stretch of highway just outside of Jefferson City, Missouri is notoriously haunted. On both side of the road is cornfields and when people travel here at night, they claim that a light strange light will follow them for four to five miles at a time. Locals claim an old man named Olfie haunts the road.

Some have gotten out of their cars at night because they believe that they have run into a person along the road. They search all over but cannot find a body. If you turn around at this point and head back in the opposite direction, some have been chasing by an unknown weird creature.

There are two bridges that exist on Old Highway 94. Finding the second bridge isn't very easy but this is the haunted one. During the Civil War, an entire family of abolitionists was hung on the bridge, even the children. The sounds of screams can be heard quite loudly at night, as well as children laughing and the vision of what looks like small wet footprints appearing in front of cars near the bridge have been reported.

Joplin 64801

Spooklight Road

Perhaps one of the most famous ghost lights ever reported, it's been called by many names, including The Tri-State Spooklight, and many neighboring communities claim the light as their own such as Neosho, Joplin, Hornet, Seneca and Quapaw, Oklahoma. Allegedly first encountered during the infamous Trail of Tears in 1836, the light was officially first reported in 1881, according to a publication published by Foster Young entitled *Ozark Spooklight*.

The Spooklight is actually seen and encountered in Oklahoma near the town of Quapaw, because the best viewing point is on the Missouri-Oklahoma border and the light is truly in the state of Oklahoma and hasn't made many treks into the state of Missouri.

Legends are many for the possible cause, including one of the oldest handed down by the Quapaw Indians who live nearby. They tell of two young Indian lovers who wished to marry but the chief demanded a usually large amount for his daughter's hand. Unable to meet his demand, they decided to elope against the chief's wishes. A war party was soon dispatched once the two were discovered missing. They both knew if they were captured, the punishment would be harsh for their deed and they decided to commit suicide by leaping together from the top of a high bluff overlooking nearby Spring River. The light that is now seen is said to be the spirits of the young lovers brought together in death.

In the 1870 era, another legend told of a miner whose cabin was raided by Indians while he was away. His wife and children were taken captive and he never saw them again. He is allegedly still searching for them with his lantern. And, of course, there is a legend concerning a farmer who was captured by Indians and beheaded. His lantern light is still seen along the road looking for his disembodied head!

The very first recorded investigation of the Spooklight was in 1942 by a group of students from the University of Michigan. They cam away completely mystified and without any answers. Next, the United States Army Corp of Engineers from nearby Camp Crowder began their research and studies of the phenomena in 1946. However, Capt. R.L. Loftin, in charge of the study later believed engineers had used the wrong road.

Around 1945, Dr. George W. Ward, formerly of the National Bureau of Standards, made some first-hand observations of the light and basically said, about the possibility that the lights were nothing more than headlights, that "the relative humidity and temperature would have to attain the correct values to produce the correct density of atmosphere to bend the light sufficiently for observation."

In the fall of 1955, a group of students from Shawnee Mission, Kansas High School looked into the light. The group was assisted by Loftin. Again no concrete answers were found.

One geologist theorized that the Spooklight might be some kind of "electrical emanation from ore beneath the ground." In other words, some form of piezoelectric effect. Another individual looked through binoculars and was sure that it was a light on top of a gravel pile. Really!

The Ghost Research Society first investigated this location on Labor Day weekend in 1982. We were able to get some outstanding pictures and video of this light and have some close encounters of our own but came up with no explainable answers.

While observing the light with a group of fellow researchers during that trip, we suddenly stepped into what can best be described as a "Zone of Fear"; a small, self-contained space where we felt a sudden, uncontrollable panic or anxiety attack. All we wanted to do at that point was to get in our cars and drive quickly away, however as we took a few steps backward, we all felt fine. Again talking a few steps forward again and the bizarre paranoia returned.

All this happened while we were observing the light through high-powered binoculars. The light was not on the road at this time but observed slightly off the road and near a barn. The light was so intensely bright that we thought the barn was on fire.

It stayed in that relative position for about thirty seconds and then slowly disappeared behind a hill. What was truly remarkable was the space that was just occupied a moment ago by this enigma, now twinkled and glowed with some form of luminosity or phosphorescence. It quite literally sparkled with energy like so many fireflies buzzing around!

It then reappeared in that same location twice more, bobbing up and down like a fisherman's cork on the water, before disappearing altogether. We crept silently up the hill in the car hoping to see where it had gone but before we got to the crest of the hill, it suddenly reappeared in the middle of the road ahead of us less than seventy yards away! The light then proceeded to perform the now famous "bobbing action' before disappearing after the third appearance. We attempted to crest the hill as quickly as possible but as we reached the summit, the light was already an estimated mile and half away in the distance treetops. Total elapsed time to arrive at the summit was no more than sixty seconds!

The GRS has returned many other times to investigate the light; May 1983 and the most thorough investigation to date was in June 2002 where we employed the latest in high technology.

To reach this location from Joplin take I-44 west to State Road 43 south, to Road BB west, follow the road until you come to a T in the road and turn right. The first road on the left is Spooklight Road and the best place for observations.

Marceline 64658

Rt. 36

Just east of the town there is a railroad bridge that crosses Rt. 36. At that bride, numerous eyewitnesses have reported seeing a misty white figure hovering just above the road. The apparition has been seen near or on the bridge and sometimes under the bridge as well. Many times the figure will disappear just before you get to it while other times people actually claim to have driven through the apparition! No one seems to know who this is or what it represents.

Poplar Bluff 63901

Wilcox Road & railroad tracks

To reach these railroad tracks one must travel down Wilcox Road (Co. Rd. 554) until you come to a fork in the road, take that to the left and follow it until you reach the railroad crossing. It is said if you arrive between the hours of 10pm and Midnight you will see spirits there.

A local legend says that back in the early 1900s there was a tragic train crash that killed most of its passengers. Allegedly there were some weird things once the accident investigation got underway including a pregnant woman whose baby was missing from her womb and a gentleman who was decapitated and his head was never found.

When you arrive at the location, you pull up to the tracks, shut off your car and allegedly the inside windows will quickly fog up and you just might hear a train whistle in the distance. It continues to get louder and louder then suddenly stops altogether. Others have seen a light that appears to be coming down the tracks. Some have claimed to have heard a tapping on their window and when they look out, they see a figure of a woman asking where her baby is.

Another story whether or not it is related to the train wreck is told of a beautiful girl with long brown flowing hair that has been seen walking towards cars wearing a long white sleeveless wedding dress and carrying a water bucket. She is said to look like an Indian woman. Locals believe that the ghost is that of the spirit of Charity taking water to the thirsty out there at night.

Raytown 64133

Rickey Road
Rickey Road is a small street that sits on what is now the old part of Noland Road. It is a very curvy road that runs through forest preserves and has no street lights. Reports vary but many have seen an apparition of a woman near a small cemetery stretching out her arms towards passing motorists. She has been described as wearing a wedding dress and a veil but when they return either later or the next day to get another glimpse of her; they find no such cemetery but a house under construction and a wide open field on the other side.

Another person claimed to have encountered a head with a terrified look on its face come rolling out from the woods, towards and then under passing cars. When they get out of their car to investigate, they find nothing at all!

Just before you come to an old dilapidated bridge, a number of signs on the side of the road have been painted with the word Murder. People have heard something walking on the bridge on two legs but nothing is seen visually.

Springfield 65806

Brooks Phelps Grove Park Bridge
This bridge is located at the intersection of 5 National Ave and East Bennett Street in Springfield, Missouri. It is a bridge made out of concrete and medium to small-sized rocks.

Under the third bridge in Phelps Grove Park many have seen a woman in a wedding dress at night known by locals as the "Bride under the Bridge." Allegedly she was killed on her wedding day. Some even claim that on moonlit evenings, one can even see the shape of the bride's hear and veil silhouetted in the rocks.

Union 63084

Union Covered Bridge

Union Covered Bridge State Historic Site in Monroe County, Missouri is maintained by the Missouri Department of Natural Resources. The bridge was built in 1871 by Joseph C. Elliot across the Elk Fork of the Salt River. In 1968 a partial restoration was completed using materials from the Mexico Covered Bridge which was destroyed the year before by flood waters. In 1970 the bridge was closed after structural timbers were damaged by overweight trucks. A total restoration was completed in 1988 and the bridge was placed on the National Register of Historic Places in 1970.

Legends abound of a death of a little boy in the mid 1800s that fell and drowned in the river. At night people claim to see the apparition of that little boy who attempts to reach out and touch people who walk across the bridge at night.

From Paris, follow Hwy 15 and the signs to the bridge.

Washington 63090

Enoch's Knob Road Bridge

Enoch's Knob Road Bridge spans Beouf Creek along a rural dirt road outside of Washington, Missouri at +38.5783, -91.1458. The road runs from State Highway 185 to the creek and then parallels State Highway 100 which is approximately a mile north of the bridge. The bridge is 185 long and 15 feet wide and has been deemed structurally unsound.

There is a heavy metal plate on the bridge today that was allegedly placed there after a child fell through a hole on the deck. This cannot be confirmed through newspaper accounts however. Allegedly there was a suicide on the bridge in 1987 however according to research conducted by *Full Moon Paranormal Society*, his family said the man was climbing the bridge while on prescription medication from a recent hip surgery and actually fell to his death.

In 2005 there was a murder of a man in the parking area near the bridge apparently due to a drug deal. After he was shot, his body was shoved under the car and it was set afire!

Reports of the feelings of presences due to the untimely deaths have been felt by many who have visited the bridge at night. Other more bizarre reports include that of an apparition of a gnome with red glowing eyes which has been observed climbing up a dead tree near the bridge.

NEBRASKA

Darr 69130

Darr Bridge

Darr Bridge located in Dawson County at 40.7747288, -99.8523412 near Darr, Nebraska.

It is said if you cross this bridge near midnight in winter when the fog is heavy, you might catch a glimpse of an apparition of a woman dressed in the period of the pioneer days in your rearview mirror. Some claim that she is riding in a covered wagon and looking for her son that died nearby.

Weeping Water 68463

Witch's Bridge

To find this obscure bridge, take Eldora Avenue out of town to the old mining town of Snydersville and there you will find an old wooden-planked bridge where allegedly a witch was once hanged from.

Legend says if you visit the bridge on an odd night with an odd amount of people, and hang your head and the top half of your body over the side of the bridge, you will see yourself hanging with a noose wrapped tightly around your neck. However, some say use caution if you try this, because the ghost of the old witch might just pull you under the bridge and you may fall to your death.

Cpl. Justina Barnhart of the Cass County Sheriff's Department has heard of the bridge and grew up by the area as a youngster herself. She says the reason it's called "Witch's Bridge" is that an elderly lady was working along the tracks one day and was hit by a train and killed. Supposedly that is why her spirit stays there to this very day. However she also believes that the real Witch's Bridge may be a much smaller one about a mile west of this bridge. Locals know for sure which one is the real haunt.

NEW JERSEY

Allamuchy 07820

Shades of Death Road

Shades of Death Road is a two-lane rural road about seven miles in length in central Warren County, New Jersey. It was named by locals due to all the deaths and accidents along this road and due to the tree-line shading the road.

In the 1920s and 1930s there were three murders along the road, one robbery where a man was hit over the head with a tire iron over gold coins, the second in which a woman beheaded her husband and buried the head and body on opposite sides of the road, and a local resident, Bill Cummins, who was shot and buried.

Along Shades of Death Road lies Ghost Lake in the Jenny Jump State Forest south of the I-80 overpass. It was given the name due to the wraithlike vapor formations often seen rising off it on cooler mornings. *Weird NJ Magazine* writes that visitors have told them that no matter what time of night they visit the lake at, the sky above it always seems as bright as if it were still twilight and several have reported ghosts in the area, especially in a deserted old cabin across the lake from the road, supposedly victims of murders once believed to have given the road its name.

Just to the right of Ghost Lake, there is a small cave once used by the Lenape Indians. The cave while covered today with graffiti was surveyed and explored in 1918 and archaeologists discovered pottery shards, flint and broken arrow heads. Known as The Fairy Hole today wasn't often visited by the Lenape but may have held great sacred or religious significance to them.

The Ghost Research Society along with New Jersey State Coordinator Randy Liebeck visited these locations in June of 1999. What happened to us was a little confusing and a bit frightening as we could not figure out how to get back onto the main highway. It was almost like stepping into *The Twilight Zone*! Even Mr. Liebeck, who had been there several times in the past, was getting a bit concerned and worried as we just continued to see the same scenery over and over again. Finally after several hours of driving around, we were able to make it back out to the main road.

Hibernia 07842

Split Rock Road

There are numerous legends surrounding this stretch of road. One such urban legend goes: if you drive down this road late at night, people (who these people are depends on who you're talking to locally), they might be Satanists/Albinos/Gangs, will block each end of the one-lane bridge and trap you in the middle as you drive across it. There have been murders and suicides on this road. Animal carcasses have been found as well as unexplained lights in the sky.

This road runs from Green Pond Road to the north of Denville.

Moorestown 08057

McElwee Road

The McElwee family lived on a large estate in New Jersey, where is now called Moorestown, in the late 1800's. Jonathan McElwee and his wife, Lucille, were very wealthy. They made their money from the railroad industry. During the time that Jonathan and his wife lived in their mansion, they had a child Jacob. When Jacob was eight years old, his mother became pregnant again. The family was overjoyed with the news and Jacob couldn't wait until his sibling was born. The day came when the baby was to be delivered in the mansion, which was not unusual for the time. As the baby was born, at 11:11pm, the family noticed something terribly wrong. The child had died during birth. This was a big shock to the family and Lucille locked herself in the attic for days after this event. She went mad and blamed her younger son, Jacob, for the death of her baby. One day, Jonathan McElwee had to leave the home for business. The mother took Jacob to the family pond behind the mansion and drowned him, at 11:11pm, since that is when the baby died. Later, when the father returned, the mother was hung for her crimes and Jacob was buried in the family plot to the right of their home. After this terrific incident, the father couldn't bare to look at the house, so he tore it down. During the deconstruction, the men that were hired to destroy the house also accidentally destroyed Jacob's grave stone. After much searching, the father could not find the body. After the mansion was gone, the town put a road up going directly through where the great estate once stood. They named the road McElwee Rd. in memory of the family. It is said that the boy's body was never found and haunts the road every night at 11:11pm. Many say to have seen him in the open field pointing to the spot where his body is buried. Others say that he is walking around the pond, which is still their today.

In order to find this road, you must go down Hartford Rd. in Moorestown, NJ. If you are coming from Rt.130, then you make a left on McElwee (it is between Cox Rd. and Borton Landing). When you turn down the street, go down a little and you can see the family pond on your left (the place where Jacob was murdered). Now, creep down the road and look for the last street light on the right side of the road. Next to the last street light is a field where the family plot once was (where Jacob's body was never found and still said to be). This road goes directly through where the McElwee Manor once stood. Once you get to the street light, drive about 20 feet farther down the road, and turn off your car. This is so you have the chance to see the boy. Just sit there until 11:11pm with your car turned off. You will either see Jacob pointing towards his body's final resting place, or he will be walking down the road from the pond.

(Credit: Haunted Road, www.freewebs.com/hauntedroad/)

New Monmouth 07748

Shelly Drive

The housing project that now lines Shelly Drive was once a flourishing grove of trees during the Revolutionary War and provided cover and shelter to both sides during the fighting there. Right where Shelly Drive ends today into the subdivision, there was a large engagement between British and American troops where many were killed.

William Champlain was a soldier of the Patriots but was also a spy for the British. Washington's troops later discovered this but did not let Champlain know that he had been compromised. At the beginning of the fight the word was given by Washington that Champlain should be shot from behind instead of warranting a firing squad. As he moved towards the front of the column, a volley of bullets rang out from the Patriots and Champlain was dead.

Many believe that the ghost of William Champlain not haunts that subdivision in order to discover the reason he was shot by his own troops. He was only seventeen when he died and very fond of his flute. Some have heard the gentle strains of flute music in the vicinity as well.

West Milford 07480

Clinton Road

Clinton Road is located in West Milford, New Jersey, Passaic County and runs for twenty-three miles in a north-south direction from Rt. 23 to Upper Greenwood Lake.

This location is probably one of the most famous haunted locations next to the *Jersey Devil* in New Jersey and has allegedly been the seen of Klu Klux Klan sightings, numerous paranormal sightings of ghosts, strange creatures, satanic worship sites, gathering of witches and even allegedly killers disposing of their victims along the road.

At one of the bridges that span Clinton Brook near the reservoir, legend has it that if throw a penny (some say a quarter) over the bridge at midnight, it will be thrown back at you! Allegedly a child was walking along the road one evening when a speeding car came around a corner too quickly, hit and killed him. He fell over the bridge and died.

A ghost car has been seen by many on Clinton Road. It has been described as a Camaro driven by a young girl who crashed it in 1988. If you bring up this story when driving down Clinton Road, it allegedly spawns this ghost car apparition.

Other phantom vehicles have also been seen, namely ghost trucks that apparently appear out of nowhere and chase other vehicles down the road before mysteriously disappearing completely!

Other claims include people coming into contact with two park rangers near Terrace Pond. The only weird thing is that no real park rangers were actually there and it is thought that what people are experiencing are really the ghosts of those two that died back in 1939.

There have even been unusual reports of strange creatures, some fringing on hybrids roaming the area at night. Hellhounds, monkeys and unidentifiable creatures have been reported since 1976 and some believe that they are survivors from a now defunct nearby attraction once called, Jungle Habitat. Those with a very vivid imagination believe that some animals might have escaped and even cross-bred with other species henceforth these weird hybrids.

All in all, a very weird and scary place to visit at night!

NEW MEXICO

Los Alamos 87545

Peggy Sue Bridge
This was an actual pipeline and footbridge with a span of 550 feet spanning Acid Canyon but was removed in February of 1997.

An urban legend states that a young girl named Peggy Sue was so depressed that she jumped from the bridge to her death back in the 1950s. Allegedly her ghost still lingers around the site. It was a tradition in the past when the bridge was still there for students from Los Alamos High School to try to cross the bridge at night; unfortunately the bridge is gone but some say there are still some remnants of the old bridge remaining to the very day.

NEW YORK

Angola 14006

Holland Road "Pigman's Road"

Pigman's Road is actually known as Holland Road and is located off NY Route 5 between Angola and the Evangola State Park. This local legend has attracted local teenagers, investigators and ordinary people alike. The bridge is located on Holland Road between Rt. 5 and Hardpan Road.

The location was the scene of a ghastly train wreck that was locally called the "Angola Horror" on December 18, 1867. Fifty people lost their lives that evening. A six-car passenger train was heading eastbound toward Buffalo and was nearing a bridge. The trailing car broke loose due to a faulty axle and plunged down the embankment as the car in front was turned on its side. Fire quickly spread on the overturned car, however all but one of the 40 plus passengers survived.

The people in the car that plunged off the embankment weren't so lucky. Two gigantic coal stoves used to heat the interior of the car broke loose and sent the fiery embers, coal and fire throughout the compartment. Before rescuers could respond to the disaster, fifty people had been burned to death!

The reason the road got the name, Pigman's Road was due to a killer over 50 years ago that used to stalk the area and road. Many said that he was a butcher and had received the name Pigman because he often displayed decapitated pigs heads on stakes throughout his yard to ward off the curious.

Allegedly one night a few teenage boys decided to spy on the Pigman to see what he was all about and that was their undoing. He caught the three boys and one by one cut off their heads while the others watched and displayed their heads on stakes in the ground. However, after this night he was never seen or heard of again.

The location is thought to be haunted by the souls of those who died in the train crash of 1867 and more recently of the Pigman's victims.

Clinton Corners 12514

Fiddler's Bridge

The original old wooden bridge is gone now and a fine, new steel structure has been built over a small tributary of Wappinger's Creek in Dutchess County near Poughkeepsie, New York.

It was there, according to old accounts, that a popular fiddler at area square dances, who had the unfortunate habit of carrying large amounts of money, was robbed and slain by a savage band of cutthroats on September 7, 1808.

Almost immediately, reports began to circulate among his surviving Hudson Valley neighbors that the restless spirit of the hapless musician had returned and was playing a ghostly fiddle by a creek.

At midnight exactly one hundred years after his death, several brave residents of the area gathered at the bridge in the gloomy light of a mist-shrouded moon. Sure enough, a few minutes after they arrived, the faint melody of the ghostly fiddle was heard.

According to an account in the Poughkeepsie Daily Eagle a few days later, some of the braver members of the group walked boldly forward toward the sound of the music. Others, less courageous, nearly swooned.

Huntington 11743

Sweet Hollow Road

Sweet Hollow Road in Huntington, New York runs from Walt Whitman Road on the south to Rt. 25 on the north and there are many local legends associated with it.

One legend deals with three youths that hung themselves from the Northern State overpass bridge. If one visits the area at night, it is said that you can occasionally see the three bodies still swaying from the bridge. There is no police record or newspaper account of this report.

The second tale is of a busload of children on their way home from school in wintery weather conditions. The bus lost control and plunged off the Northern State overpass bridge, killing them all. People claim that their car is pushed mysteriously while visiting the site. Perhaps it's the spirits of the dead children helping so that a similar accident isn't repeated. No such report or accident can be found regarding this story.

Another story is of a white lady named Mary that is said to frequent the area. Apparently she and her boyfriend were driving down Sweet Hollow Road when they got into an argument. Either she jumped or the boyfriend pushed her from the speeding car. She was killed by another car that struck her on the pavement. Some say you will see an apparition of a lady dressed in white that will jump at your car when you attempt to pass her.

A very scary account tells of a police officer that pulls over passing cars. He walks over to your car, questions the driver and always lets them go without issuing a citation. Those that look in their rearview as the officer walks away claim that the back of his head has been blown away as if with a shotgun blast. Allegedly a police officer was killed in the line of duty very near there but that story cannot be verified.

Ghost children are sometimes seen on Sweet Hollow Road. Supposedly back in the 1930s there was a day camp somewhere nearby and a lot of children were abused and killed there. When driving through the area at night, motorists might catch a glimpse of children dressed in the style of the 1930s simply walking on the side of the road before disappearing.

Montebello 10901

Spook Rock Road

There are several stories and legends relating to this strange outcropping of rock including the first regarding a Dutch settler who was accused of cheating Native American Indians in a trade. To get even, the Indians kidnapped his daughter and sacrificed her at the rock. To this very day, it is said that a ghostly white apparition can be seen floating in the area.

Another tale concerns a Dutch woman and a Native American Indian who fell in love which each other. The other Dutch settlers were outraged by this and murdered them both at the rock. There screams can still both be heard at the rock at night.

Other reports include a woman in a white Victorian gown that wanders up and down the road at night. Some claim that their automobile, once placed in neutral, will move on its own and sometimes you can actually see a ghostly figure pulling the automobile.

NORTH CAROLINA

Asheville 28801

Helen's Bridge

Helen's Bridge is located on Beaucatcher Mountain in Asheville, North Carolina. It is a spooky setting indeed and has long been associated with a lot of paranormal activity.

One such story concerns a woman who was very unhappy over the death of her death in a fire so she decided to commit suicide by hanging herself from the bridge. The ghost of Helen is supposed to be seen walking the bridge at night asking those she meets where her daughter is.

Other reports of cars mysteriously dying out at the bridge or some other kind of car problems and dark foreboding creatures that emerge from the surrounding woods. Some have reported being slapped, scratched or attacked in some way when visiting the site so caution and a good dose of bravery would be in order if you decide to travel out her at night.

Brunswick 28424

Mt. Misery Road

During the times of slavery, this road was frequently used to transport slaves to Fayetteville, almost ninety miles away. Many would not make the march and died along the way due to the oppressive heat and lack of water. However the rest continued to march, reaching their final destination and leaving the dying and dead behind.

Motorists driving along this stretch of roadway have often felt a great sense of dread or even sadness that they cannot attribute to anything else. Are they picking up on the emotions, grief and agony of those who suffered and died along this trail?

Others have sworn to have heard the sounds of chains clanking and moaning sounds but nothing is ever visible to the naked eye. Areas where strong emotions have been dumped into often can hold onto those place memories for quite sometime and people passing through those locations can indeed pick up on those residual sounds and feelings of the past.

Jamestown 27282

Lydia's Bridge

Lydia's Bridge is a vine-covered, overgrown structure near Jamestown, North Carolina and scene of a hitchhiking ghost story. A lovely young figure of a woman has been reported hitchhiking along Rt. 70 just east of town near High Point. The girl gets into the car and sometimes relates the story of an argument with her boyfriend while at a dance. She gives the driver directions to her house and upon arriving in the driveway; the girl has simply vanished from inside the car without opening the doors!

Sometimes the driver will go to the house and ring the bell, relating his experience only to be told by the parents that Lydia died on her way home from a dance in 1923!

One of the first person's to encounter this hitchhiking phantom was back in 1924. Other reports tell of seeing a pale figure of a woman standing just past the bridge or sometimes bloodcurdling screams in the night.

Lydia's Bridge is still there although it's about forty feet from the new overpass. A recent death certificate was uncovered for a Lydia Jane M. who was born in 1904 in High Point and died, December 31, 1923 due to a car crash. So perhaps the story of Lydia is more than just urban legend. Perhaps there was Lydia in real life?

Riding from Greensboro to Charlotte on I-85 South/Highway 70, take exit 118, the Jamestown/High Point exit; this is also business 85/Highway 70. Go about a mile, and get off on the first exit you come to, Jamestown/Sedgefield (the exit is not numbered). At the top of the ramp is Vickery Chapel Road; turn right at the stop sign. Go about a half a mile; you'll come to a traffic light where Vickery Chapel Road veers off to the left. Take that left, go another mile and you'll come to another traffic light, this is "High Point Road", or Main Street, depending on which sign you read. Hang a left at that light, you'll go around a bend and immediately see the railroad underpass, as well as the "Welcome to Jamestown" sign. When you go under the tracks, you'll see a turn-out spot on your right where you can park. Looking back at the underpass, you'll be able to see the old underpass there on the right, through some trees.

Smithfield 27577

Mill Creek Bridge

Dancing lights have been seen on this bridge, mostly in the 1950's. Stories say the lights are that of the ghost of an old black man who was being beaten by his cruel master. Apparently the master went too far with his lashings one day and the slave fought back, killing his master. He buried the body under the bridge and shortly thereafter strange things began happening there. As people walked over the bridge, their lanterns would go out and strange sounds came from under the bridge. This bridge is located outside Smithfield in Johnson County.

Mill Creek is six miles down 701 South from Hannah's Creek (about 14 total miles south of Smithfield on 701); at Shaw's Creek Road, take a left. In less than a mile you'll come to two Mill Creek Bridges. One of them should be THE Mill Creek Bridge.

Statesville 28677
Bostian Bridge

On August 27, 1891, a passenger train wrecked near this bridge that is located east of Statesville, NC. The train, number nine, was headed from Salisbury to Asheville when it derailed and fell off the bridge into the ravine below. A total of 30 people were killed, including the baggage master, and there were numerous injuries. Legend says this wreck is repeated annually at 3 AM on the anniversary of the disaster. Witnesses have reported hearing the sounds of twisted metal, steam pipes rupturing and the screams of the passengers. Upon investigation, there is never any evidence of an accident. Some people have reported being approached by the ghost of the baggage master of the train asking for the correct time so he can set his watch.

This bridge can be very dangerous and ghost hunting is discouraged especially after the disaster that happened on August 27, 2010.

A man who was with about a dozen people who were looking for the legendary "ghost train" was hit by a locomotive and killed. The incident happened on the train trestle at 2:45a.m. near the 900 block of Buffalo Shoals Road.

Robin Chapman, a spokesperson for Norfolk-Southern Railroad, said the eastbound train consisted of three locomotives and no freight cars. The train was rounding a curse and approaching a trestle over Boston Creek just prior to Buffalo Shoals Road when it struck a man on the trestle, Chapman said. Christopher Kaiser, 29, died at the scene and two more people were injured, according to Iredell County Sheriff Phillip Redmond. Kaiser's body was found below the trestle down a steep incline, he said. The injured patients were airlifted to a local hospital.

Redmond said there were 12 people who were amateur ghost hunters caught on the trestle when the train rounded the bend early Friday morning. The train operators tried to stop the locomotives and warn the people on the trestle. Most of the people on the trestle started running east and away from the train. All of the victims were able to clear the trestle except for the fatal victim who was struck by a locomotive.

Remember never trespass on private property. Always get permission to investigation a location and never put yourself in danger for your hobby!

NORTH DAKOTA

Leroy 58282

White Lady Road

A local legend tells of a traveling salesman who fell in love with a farmer's daughter. He took her for a walk on a remote road and made their way to a bridge to make his move. She rejected his advances, so he killed her.

Now at night, people claim to see a white-clad figure of a woman standing on the road. In an instant, the figure is seen sitting on the car staring in with red glowing eyes, apparently looking for her killer.

Another tale is completely different and concerns a farmer's daughter again but this time she gets pregnant out of wedlock and the family forces a shotgun wedding. On her wedding day, she returns home only to find the baby dead in the crib.

Quite distraught over the loss of her child and not wanting to live anymore she travels to the bridge where she hangs herself, still wearing her wedding gown. People who travel out to the bridge at night claim to see the woman still hanging there from the bridge in her wedding dress.

The bridge is located down a narrow road off County Road 9 which leads through Tetrault Woods between Leroy and Walhalla. It's sometimes called White Lady Lane.

OHIO

Amelia 45102

Dead Man's Curve

Dead Man's Curve is a dangerous intersection and windy road in Clermont County near CR 222 and State Rt. 125 meet. This was part of the Ohio Turnpike built back in 1831 and has claimed a lot of traffic victims throughout the years. In September of 1969 the State of Ohio redesigned it as a straight four-lane road but that didn't stop the accidents. On October 19, 1969, five youths perished here when their 1968 Impala was hit by a 1969 Roadrunner going in excess of one hundred miles per hour. Rick was the only survivor of this serious accident.

Ever since that awful crash, the intersection has been haunted by a faceless hitchhiker. Rick has actually seen this apparition on five different occasions. It has been described as a shadow figure; a three-dimensional silhouette.

In the book *Haunted Ohio III* by Chris Woodyard, Rick's friend Todd is quoted as saying, "Rick and I were heading home from Bethel to Amelia. I noticed a man's shape on the side of the road. It turned like it was hitchhiking, with an arm sticking up. The thing wore light-colored pants, a blue shirt, and longer hair--and there was just a blank, flat surface where the face should have been. We looked back. There was nobody there. I've also seen the black shadow figure, walking its slow, labored, dragging walk by the side of the road."

Rick's girlfriend had a frightening encounter with the apparition one evening when it threw itself of her car. She felt the tires roll over the figure so she stopped the car only to see in horror the figure trying to climb onto her car! Driverless Impalas and Roadrunners are also sometimes seen where the accident occurred as though it's some kind of ghostly reenactment of the event all over again.

Due to rerouting, the actual location of Dead Man's Curve is somewhat in doubt. They say it's at 222 and SR 125, near Bantam Road. As you head east on 125, 222 turns right towards Felicity and Bantam Road turns left toward East Fork Lake State Park. The spot is just below a carryout

Ashland 44805

Haunted Tunnel off Rt. 24
Just off Route 42 on the way to Mansfield from Ashland is a tunnel which is supposed to be haunted by a ghost or group of ghosts. They will push your car through the tunnel if you shut the engine off and put it in neutral. If you honk your horn three times you might see the hanging body of a man who killed himself there after his wife died giving birth. Their home was located near the tunnel but was burned to the ground by vandals. To find the tunnel on Rt. 42, look for the offices of an exterminating company.

Batavia 45103

Lucy Run Road
A figure in white often startles travelers on Lucy Run Road, dashing across the road to evaporate before their eyes at the gate to Batavia Cemetery. This is the story of who she is and where she came from.

The family of Charles Robinson set out for the west in 1806, first spending time in Kentucky, then settling for good in the fields of Clermont County, Ohio, building his family a log cabin alongside a sizable creek. Charles had several daughters. One of them, Lucy, was especially attractive and promising, and when she promptly became engaged at the proper age no one was surprised.

Then disaster struck. The fiancée rode to the Robinson cabin in a thunderstorm to tell her the bad news: he had met someone else, was in love with another woman. The engagement was off.

He rode off too quickly for the stunned Lucy, who mounted her horse and rode out into the storm to follow him. The rain was coming down in thick sheets, making visibility almost impossible, and somehow she missed the bridge and rode into the swollen creek.

Thrown from her horse, she was swept away immediately and drowned in the muddy water. From that time onward, the creek was known as Lucy's Run, and the road that runs alongside it Lucy Run Road. And Lucy has always been seen, running without a horse, across the road from the place where her family's homestead was to the gates of the cemetery where she is buried.

(Credit: Crawford, Rick. Uneasy Spirits: 13 Ghost Stories from Clermont County, Ohio. Rhiannon Publications, 1997. pg. 14-17.)

Byron 44122

Trebein Road

Trebein Road, near Byron in Greene County, is said to be haunted by the spirit of a woman who died when her carriage hit a rock and flung her onto the ground to break her neck on her wedding day. Her grieving father and fiancée dug the rock out and rolled it off the side of the road, where it still is today. Some say the lady in white is transparent, but most agree that she looks just like a normal woman. It's hard to say when she'll appear; some say it must be on her birthday, or the anniversary of her death, or her funeral.

Columbus

Watkins Road Bridge

The little bridge which spans a little creek on Watkins Road in southeast Columbus is said to be haunted by a woman who died in a car accident there and whose head can be seen in the trees overhead if you stop there and honk your horn three times. Another version tells of a mother who lost her baby in the icy water beneath the bridge. Still another date back to when it was a covered bridge; supposedly a girl and her boyfriend were parked inside when the boyfriend decided to carve their initials in the wood. After he finished he was struck by a speeding car and killed. After that, you could go to the bridge at night and, if you were lucky, see the carving glow and hear the sound of the girlfriend's sobs.

Dayton

Bessie Little Bridge

The ghost of a murdered girl named Bessie Little returns regularly to this bridge on Ridge Street. She was murdered there on August 27, 1896, by her boyfriend, Albert J. Frantz. Bessie was pregnant and Albert didn't want to have to marry her, so he shot her in the head and arranged the scene to suggest a suicide. For some reason, however, he shot her twice, so it was obvious that she hadn't done it to herself. On November 19, 1897, Albert J. Frantz #28896 was strapped into the electric chair at the Ohio Penitentiary in Columbus and put to death for first degree murder. Back in Montgomery County, Bessie Little's ghost continues to haunt the bridge.

Fremont 43420

Tindall Bridge

      Tindall Bridge, often misspelled as Tindle Bridge, is located in Sandusky County Ohio near Fremont on County Road 209 (+41.30833, -83.15833). It spans the Sandusky River and was built in 1915 by the Champion Iron Company.

      This bridge is allegedly haunted by a ghost of someone who was murdered back in the 1950s. The female apparition is heard sobbing and asking for help. Sometimes she is seen under the bridge. No one seems to know if this is a true story or another urban legend but supposedly there was another murder several years ago very close to bridge in an open field, so there could be more than one ghost here.

Gratis 45330

Brubaker Bridge

Brubaker Bridge was built in 1887 and spans Sam's Run Creek. To get to this bridge, leave Gratis heading west on Route 122, then turn left onto Township Road 328.

Back in the 1930s a tragic car accident involving several teenagers happened here while they were traveling back from Grange Hall after a party. They missed a curve in the road and struck the side of the bridge and the car plunged into Sam's Run Creek. Being that this was quite desolate country back then, nobody heard or saw the accident. It wasn't discovered until a farmer from a nearby farm came out to check on his cattle that were a bit restless. Upon seeing the accident, he called authorities and an ambulance was dispatched. All were dead and transported.

The farmer and his family had terrible dreams about the accident for months and driving home late one evening from meeting, his car died out in the middle of the bridge. They both heard a series of loud raps on the windshield and hood of their car to be followed by a hissing sound like rushing water or wind. A few seconds later, they car came to life and they drove home. Apparently that has happened to a lot of other people since that day.

Allegedly one body was never found from the accident to this day. Apparently the ghost of the missing boy is the one who messes with cars crossing the bridge from time to time in an attempt to find his missing body and give him a proper burial.

Lancaster (Clearport) 43130

Johnston Bridge

Johnston Covered Bridge (often misspelled Johnson) is also known as Terry Mill Bridge was built in 1887 and is located ESE of Clearport, Ohio on Amanda/Clearport Road (CR 69). The GPS location is Lat. 39.6135N & Long. -82.6595W. The bridge has been retired from service and is not used anymore for any traffic; it's just a historic site.

Long before it was retired an apparition of a woman was said to haunt the bridge but nobody seems to know who she is or why she stays at the bridge. Some say she fell into Clear Creek and drowned while attempting to guide horses through the bridge during a severe thunderstorm.

Another version claims that her husband was unfaithful and she killed herself by either jumping to her death or hanging herself from the structure. Many have seen her beckoning to them.

Mansfield 44903

Reformatory Road

The road that runs adjacent to Mansfield Reformatory is also haunted by the ghost of Phoebe Wise who was a bit of an eccentric. Her home was located on what was once called Olivesburg Road. The farmhouse was ordinary enough but held a commanding view of the prison and the city from Hancock Heights.

People say the Phoebe began to lose her mind and starting talking to animals of all kinds. The rear of her house started to collapse but she still continued to live there because she said she couldn't afford to fix it even though her father, Christian Wise, was a very prominent citizen of Mansfield.

Phoebe was born in 1850 to Christian and Julia Wise but no one is absolutely sure of the year. She was the youngest of eight children and did very well in school well eventually she taught music and English by the age of fourteen.

Her father died in 1887 and the mother just four years later. The estate was divided up among the children including the sale of over half of the farm. Phoebe decided to remain with the other half which lead people to believe that she was stashing an enormous amount of money somewhere in the dilapidated building.

Finally hoodlums broke into her decaying farmhouse on December 23, 1891. She heard her noises in her living room, went to investigate and was confronted by three masked men who had pistols and demanded money. They tied her to a chair and tortured her by burning her feet with a torch. She turned over a watch, gold chain and about $500 in cash which was all the fortune that was in the house. After freeing herself, she called police and

Eventually Phoebe died March 13, 1933 and some say that her ghost can be seen walking down Reformatory Road in front of the prison, headed toward Rt. 545, dressed in the clothing that people remember seeing her in during better times for Phoebe Wise.

Overton 44691

Leroy's Bridge

Leroy's Bridge near Overton is apparently haunted by a man who fell off the bridge and drowned in the creek.

One story says that Leroy was a black man that was lynched by the KKK in the 1920s for flirting with a white woman. He was hung from a tree by the bridge to discourage others from doing the same thing. After returning a few days later, the body was gone and all that remained was the noose dangling from the tree. People have seen a black man walking around the bridge and strange mysterious ghost lights are often encountered as well.

There are also rumors of ritualistic cults that use this bridge for sacrifices and Satan worship. To find this bridge, travel down Overton Road off of Rt. 604 and go south, there's a 90 degree turn just before the bridge and it is approximately two miles or so from Rt. 604.

Oxford 45056

Buckley Road

To find the exact place to perform this ritual, take Rt. 732 north out of Oxford and turn left onto the first country road, Buckley Road. Drive to the place where the road bends, turn your car around and face Rt. 732.

Now it is said if you turn the engine off, flash your lights three times, you might see a white light in the distance come toward your car from across the hills. Supposedly this is the ghost of a phantom bicyclist who was struck and killed while riding on either Buckley Road or Rt. 732.

Shunk

Turkeyfoot Creek Bridge

Turkeyfoot Creek Bridge is actually called Precht Bridge and was built by the Massillon Bridge Company and is located on Elton Road in Shelby County Ohio at +40.32167, -84.05500. The name for the bridge comes from a relatively new plaque on the bridge commemorating William Precht who died at this bridge in a tractor accident. The bridge is located within a state park and although the bridge is not restored and on an undeveloped trail, it remains open for pedestrian and horse traffic.

The legend states that travelers from Malinta might encounter the ghost of an Indian warrior riding a white stallion along the creek on the right side of the bridge. Supposedly he is protecting his loot of $40,000 in gold that was buried on the south bank of the creek.

Sugar Grove 43155

Hummell Bridge

Hummel Bridge is often associated with a phenomenon known as the blue light haunting. The bridge is located on Hansley Road and spans Rush Creek. It was originally a covered bridge at one time.

Back in the 1930s legend says a murder took place at the bridge which may have been the catalyst of the hauntings. A woman from nearby Sugar Grove visited the site, a typical lover's lane setting, with her boyfriend one evening. They were always getting into arguments and the woman had had enough and pulled a knife from her purse and proceeded to slit his throat from ear to ear and then completely decapitated him.

She then took his head to a hill just west of the bridge and engrossed it in a long conversation before slitting her own throat as well. Authorities found her body along with her boyfriend the next day.

Since that bloody murder suicide, she is said to appear on moonless nights near the bridge. If you call her by name, (either Mary or Anna), she will appear in a glowing blue light. She is also seen wandering around the hills sometimes carrying a head!

OKLAHOMA

Oklahoma City

Kitchen Lake Bridge

The legend of Kitchen Lake Bridge is that a very long time ago a witch lived in a wooden house with a stone chimney right before the intersection of SE 119th and South Air Depot where Air Depot comes to an end. Years ago the house caught fire and all that remains are the chimney and fireplace. People have reported seeing smoke coming from the fireplace from time to time.

If one drives another two miles or so down the road, you might come across 10-12 piles of garbage, toys, clothes, ceiling tiles, wood, glass and several more. Not really sure what this is supposed to represent but they have some connection it is said to the witch. People report weird things hanging from trees and animals with no heads. Sometimes car headlights will flicker and other times completely go off without any reason. There is a general feeling of foreboding and uneasiness as though a great many eyes are watching you. The sounds of footsteps can sometimes be heard following you if you are real quiet but there is nothing there making those noises.

Reports of unexplained fogs appearing out of nowhere and electrical discharges like St. Elmo's fire has been encountered. Mysterious figures and a runaway horse have been spotted in the past.

To reach this area, take I-240 and I-35. Go east to Sooner RD (77H) go south to 119th (there's a sign that says 'Firstep'. Then, turn Left (East) and it is located about 500 ft to the west of Air Depot on the north side.

Quapaw 74363

Spooklight Road
(See Missouri: Joplin, Spooklight Road)

Sand Springs 74063

Cimarron Turnpike

It seems that the Sand Springs ghost light is a well-researched, established phenomenon. The September 27, 1954 issue of the *Tulsa World* carries a write-up on the Sand Springs ghost light. Although it is not an AP report it is apparently the report that the AP picked up.

The articles states that the light had appeared for five consecutive nights at 12:05 a.m. It was described as a "fiery blue-green object with a phosphorescent glow. It would remain stationary at one spot for a while, go out, and then reappear a second later at least 200 yards away. It reportedly appears in the east and streaks westward at incredible speed." One woman claimed to have heard the light scream. Another witness said the light "started out as green then turned red then white." Sand Springs Police Chief Jack Daniels said he thought it was either a piece of metal on the hillside reflecting the moonlight of "fox fire" (luminescent fungi). Daniels said as many as 150 cars were parked along the highway nightly with their occupants gazing skyward.

The next day's *Tulsa World*, for September 28, 1954, continued a report that apparently the AP didn't pick up. Its headline read "Ghost Light at Sand Springs Fades: Teen-age Pranksters Are Unmasked."

Two teen-age boys admitted to highway patrol deputies early that morning, at the scene of the ghost light sightings, that the whole thing was a practical joke started to impress their girl friends. For the past five nights, the boys had disguised a flashlight with a green cloth and ran through the underbrush. The boys were going to repeat their performance the morning of the 28th, but became scared when people carrying guns showed up to see the light. "Both boys' legs were badly scratched where they had raced across the face of the mountain in the brambles and rocks to carry out their scheme."

The entire event was a hoax, but the resolution of the case appeared only in a local newspaper. The moral is: always check as close as possible to the original source when researching paranormal activity, and always check a few issues after the first appearance of the report.

OREGON

Culver

Old Highway 97

Along Old Highway 97 in the high desert of Oregon in between the city of Culver and the Crooked Creek Bridge, there have been numerous reports of ghosts walking along the road at night. Ghostly animals, namely cows, have suddenly appeared in the middle of the road displaying red glowing eyes. There isn't enough time to stop or slow down in time to avoid hitting the animals but that doesn't matter because your car passes right through them as if they're not really there at all!

Use caution if you plan to visit this area as the road is very treacherous and it can be very windy. There have been numerous traffic accidents which probably have contributed to the ghostly assortment of apparitions seen in the area.

Salem

Crossian Creek Road

At the intersection of Crossian Creek Road South and Kuebler Blvd a little girl was killed by a speeding car. Today some eyewitnesses report when they approach that intersection they see a ball rolling into the road followed by a little girl chasing it. Perhaps this is how she died in reality and is still reliving her last moments on earth. Most have experienced this event on Friday nights, apparently the day of the week she died.

Motorists who approach that intersection without slowing down or are speeding have often seen an apparition of a young boy standing on the side of the road wagging his finger at them in a warning for them to slow down, however when glancing in their rearview mirror, he has vanished into thin air.

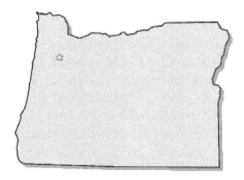

PENNSYLVANIA

Altoona 16602

Beulah Road

This road in the Wopsonock Mountains is haunted by a spectral phantom female hitchhiking ghost for a number of years. At one time there was a hotel on top of Wopsonock Mountain that was a favorite getaway for many from nearby Altoona; however the hotel burned to the ground in the early part of the last century and no effort was ever made to rebuild the place. A beautiful overlook known as Wopsy Lookout was also part of the gorgeous backdrop to this very comfortable location.

Juniata Gap Road in Altoona is the road one uses to reach the lookout and it is quite treacherous and steep with a curve aptly named "Devil's Elbow" where a number of fatal accidents have occurred throughout the years.

One legend tells of a couple heading to the hotel for their honeymoon in the early part of the 20th century when their carriage went over the edge of Devil's Elbow and both were killed however the body of the husband was never discovered.

Since that disaster, people traveling on this road have encountered a ghost of woman dressed in white, sometimes carrying a candle, and apparently looking for something. Variations of the story indicate that she sometimes peers into the windows of passing cars, looking for her missing husband or actually getting in the cars only with younger men but then disappears near the Devil's Elbow.

Gettysburg 17325

Sach's Bridge

     Sach's Bridge located near the Gettysburg Battlefield was built in 1854 by David Stoner. Sach's Covered Bridge spans Marsh Creek in Cumberland Township, Adams County, Pennsylvania and is 100' long. During the Battle of Gettysburg, the right flank of the Confederate Army of Northern Virginia artillery line was stationed and which participated in the massive barrage of cannon fire prior to Pickett's Charge on July 3, 1863. It was also used during the Confederate retreat back to Virginia beginning on July 4, 1863 however during the Civil War it was known as Sauck's Bridge.

     To find the bridge, take the Emmetsburg pike by the Visitors Center, past the Peach Orchard and make a right onto Millerstown Road. Millerstown Road will turn into Pumping Station road. Stay on Pumping station road and cross over Marsh Creek until you see the Sachs Bridge sign that is posted here. The sign will be on your left. Make a left and the bridge is about 100 yards straight ahead!

     Some of stories often told of Sach's Bridge include three Confederate deserters that were caught and hung from the bridge for their punishment. People who visit the location at night claim to feel cold spots on the bridge and photographs on digital cameras often show "orbs" and strange mist.

Then there is the carriage accident of one Peggy Noel who was apparently decapitated at the bridge. Usually in the spring of the year around dusk, fishermen wading in Marsh Creek hear the sounds of very rhythmic splashing and think it could be another fisherman approaching them but none is ever seen. Sometimes a headless apparition accompanies the sounds in the water or what has been described as a faceless specter.

Girard 16417

Gudeonville Bridge

The Gudeonville Covered Bridge was built in 1868 by William Sherman and spans Elk Creek in Girard Township, Erie County, Pennsylvania. It was listed on the National Register of Historic Places on September 17, 1980 but unfortunately was destroyed by arson on November 8, 2008. While the bridge is still standing, it's not safe to cross or stand on today.

Allegedly some forty years ago or so a little girl fell off the cliff next to the bridge, "Ox's Bow" to her death and many have seen her apparition on the bridge. Unexplained screams are also sometimes heard apparently from the girl and others that have allegedly fell to their deaths from the cliff.

Another legend tells of a man named Gudeon, named for the bridge, beat his mule to death because it refused to cross the bridge. From time to time, the sounds of hooves could be heard on the wooden planks and the baying of a mule being whipped.

Yet another story is told about a mule having a heart attack on the bridge after being spooked by a calliope playing on a barge going down a nearby canal. The name of the mule was Gudeon and permission was given to bury him on the west bank of the bridge. So whether you believe the man or mule story or either, there are some interesting stories to be told.

The bridge was later removed intact to a field and another bridge was placed there to avoid a long detour for travelers. The location is between Beckman and Francis Road in a valley overlooking a gorge known as the Devil's Punchbowl along the Elk Creek.

Montandon 17850

Rishel Covered Bridge

Rishel Covered Bridge (also known as Montandon Bridge) was built in 1830 by John Shriner and Zacheus Braley using the Burr Arch design; it has a structure length of 121 ft. and crosses the Chillisquaque creek. The bridge is located on Route # T573 east of Montandon, Pennsylvania at N40 57.63 W76 48.92 The bridge has the distinction of being the oldest covered bridge in the state of Pennsylvania. The bridge was reconstructed in 1982 and is open to traffic.

The legend surrounding this particular bridge concerns multiple murders of children by a man. When people visit this location at night and go to the center of the bridge, you are supposed to sprinkle baby powder all over the car and wait for approximately ten minutes with no lights on. In the total darkness, you can see dark shadows flitting about and after the ten minutes is up, drive to a well lit area and you should be able to see the fingerprints of all the murdered children on your car!

New Hope 18938

Van Sant Bridge

The Van Sant Bridge also called the Beaver Dam Bridge is located in Solebury Township near New Hope in Bucks County, Pennsylvania. The bridge was built in 1875 and spans the Pidcock Creek near Washington Crossing State Park.

There are numerous legends surrounding the bridge being haunted including hearing a baby crying around midnight and strange figures hanging from the rafters. Allegedly horse thieves were hung from this spot as punishment for their crimes. Strange sounds, handprints appearing on your car and the appearance of orbs and unusual mists have all been reported in the past.

Wexford 15090

Blue Myst Road

Blue Myst Road is the local name of Irwin Road, a closed roadway that runs between the town of Wexford and North Park, Pennsylvania.

There are many local legends and stories associated with most haunted site including that somewhere along Irwin Road was a rallying point for a local KKK chapter and even a hanging tree for the unfortunate who were captured by the clan. There is a foundation of a house back there that some say belonged to a witch and allegedly another house out there was called The Midget House once lived in by a race of small people who used to chase away the curious and trespassers to the area at night.

One story concerns a jealous husband that caught his wife cheating on him and he killed her and his children and dumped their bodies in a septic tank in the mid-1900s. Their spirits have been seen frequently the room from time to time.

Reports of a spectral dog and a more bizarre figure of a half-deer, half-human mutant that haunts the door as well. The Pittsburgh Ghost Hunters found all the usual stories and rumors to be false, but spotted an orb the size of a softball floating around, changing speeds and radiating a glow for at least a minute, a long time for that sort of phenomena.

SOUTH CAROLINA

Dillion 29536

Bingham's Light off I-95

(Direction: In Dillion off I-95 Dillion exit and at the Historical Marker is a dirt road that leads into the woods. Park and walk about a mile.)

It is said that after you park your car at this site, you should walk about a mile into the woods and begin yelling for the light to appear. You will know when you are close to seeing the light because the temperature will drop. It is also close to Reedy Creek Springs.

According to legend, John Bingham was hit by a train in the late 1800s or early 1900s, depending who you ask in town. He was flagging the train with a lantern and apparently it's his lantern that is still seen today swaying back and forth. The train tracks no longer exist.

One report claims that the light got to within three feet of the onlooker and he got violently ill, another claims his engine blew up when the light got too close and still another claims to have shot at the light with a rifle. The light split and changed into different colors.

Greenville 29601

Poinsett Bridge

Poinsett Bridge was built in 1820 and named for Joel Roberts Poinsett who is credited for bringing the poinsettia flower to the United States. It was part of a road (old Hwy 25N) in between Columbia, South Carolina and Saluda Mountain. The bridge is made entirely of stone but is no longer used at all but still in good condition for its age. The bridge is part of the120 acre Poinsett Bridge Heritage Preserve. It spans the Little Gap Greek, a small tributary of the North Saluda River.

A great number of ghost groups have investigated this site and have mixed conclusions as to whether the site is haunted or not. Some of the groups have reported mists, strange lights, sightings of figures and other strange anomalies in their pictures during their investigation of the bridge.

Locals have reported hearing voices near the site, seen full-bodied apparitions, strange lights and heard unexplainable noises and sounds. Other legends include that of a slave being hung from underneath the bridge and that his ghost still haunts it today. Cars mysteriously don't start or have problems starting when you attempt to leave the location and a strange light is often seen. When the light gets very near to the observer, a disembodied scream can sometimes be heard associated with it.

Summerville 29483

Highways 27 and 61
Summerville is located northwest of Charleston along Highway 27 and Highway 61.

A mysterious light has been seen there and was first discovered in December of 1961 along what was once Sheep Island Road. According to reports by the *Charlotte News* in mid-March of 1962, the light apparently enjoyed chasing automobiles down Sheep Island Road at speeds approaching 60 mph. It was said to change colors and often like to swoop down on parked cars.

TENNESSEE

Elizabethton 37643

Smalling Bridge

Smalling Bridge, often called on various websites "The Steel Bridge" is located in Carter County, Tennessee and spans the Watauga River. It was built in 1941 by Johnson City Foundry & Machine Company Tennessee Bridge Steel Company Division of Johnson City, Tennessee. Total length is slightly over 223 feet and can be found at +36.34587, -82.28296 or CR 1011.

Quite awhile ago a couple who were dating one another decided to visit the bridge and were confronted by men who robbed them. The woman was stabbed in the confrontation and apparently died on the spot. The young man was also stabbed but managed to escape the perpetrators and run for help. He was able to stop a car on the bridge and jump into the back seat to safety.

People who now travel the bridge at night (some say only on Halloween around midnight), say that when they stop their car near the middle of the bridge a person will climb into the back seat and that you can actually see the indentation of his weight impressed into the seat!

The old steel bridge is no longer there but was demolished and a new two-lane bridge installed beside the old steel one in June 2010.

Sunbright 37872

Burnt Mill Bridge

Burnt Mill Bridge is located in Big South Fork National River and Recreation Area, Scott County, Tennessee. It was built between 1920-21 by J.I. and E.J. Foster Bridge Builders and spans the Clear Fork River and can be found at +36.38775, -84.62952.

The bridge is allegedly haunted by the apparition of a young woman murdered by her father back in the 1960s and thrown over the bridge to conceal the body. People have seen this ghost walking back and forth across the bridge looking for her father. Some have actually seen a ghostly reenactment of her being thrown over the bridge only not to make a sound at all when she hits the surface of the water.

TEXAS

Anson 79501

Bridge

There are stories told of an old metal bridge on the outskirts of town that is haunted by a hanging victim. Being that it's a metal bridge, it is loud when driven over. Wind can be heard blowing on one side of the bridge, while it is calm on the other side.

(The Shadowlands Website: www.theshadowlands.net)

There is another story told around Anson called the Anson Lights. Now whether or not this is at all related to the previous story or not, one would have to ask locals. However the Anson Lights are supposed to be a ghost of a woman from the 1800s who is looking for her lost son. Outside of Anson there is a cemetery. About a quarter of a mile down the dirt road running along side the cemetery there is a cross roads. In order to see the lights, you are supposed to go to the cross roads and turn around and then flash your lights, turn them off and wait.

Twinkling, flickering lights are then seen on the horizon that dance down the road towards the onlookers in their cars, sometimes approaching as close as fifty feet! Rumor has it if the light gets too close to your car and you become too frightened, all you need do is turn on the cars headlights and the light will mysteriously vanish.

To find this location from Abilene, take State Highway 277N 20 miles to Anson, then follow the directions listed above.

Denton 76201

Goat Man's Bridge

Goat Man's Bridge is actually called Old Alton Bridge or Copper Canyon Road Bridge and is located in Denton County, near Denton, Texas. It was built in 1884 by the King Bridge Company of Cleveland, Ohio and can be found at +33.12936, -97.10403 or Copper Canyon Road. The bridge spans Hickory Creek and is currently only open to pedestrians as a newer traffic bridge was built. It was placed on the National Register of Historic Places on July 8, 1988.

The name Goat Man's Bridge is derived from a hard working black goat farmer and his family that lived just north of the bridge at the turn of the 20th century. Oscar Washburn was a very dependable farmer and businessman who eventually was dubbed "The Goatman." However the local KKK weren't so thrilled with the success of this individual so one night in August of 1938, they broke into Washburn's house and dragged him to the bridge where they hung him.

Later looking over at their handy work, they saw a noose but no body hanging from the bridge. In a panic, they returned to the house where they murdered the rest of the family in cold blood.

Since the murders, a number of strange occurrences have happened on the bridge including sightings of the Goatman himself on occasion.

There have also been numerous missing person's reports and abandoned vehicles found in the vicinity of the bridge.

Some have claimed to have witnessed the Goatman herding his goats across the bridge in the middle of the night while others report just seeing his apparition staring at them with two goat heads, one under each arm. Even stranger tales of a half-man, half-goat have been reported by some in the past. Strange sounds like horse hoofs on the wooden planks of the bridge, splashing in the water below, laugher and growling sounds continue to this day.

Mysterious ghost lights seen on the bridge are frequently encountered, car doors which lock and unlock by themselves when traveling on the bridge and unexplained car break downs. There is also an unrelated report of a woman being seen on the bridge at night, perhaps it isn't so unrelated after all; it could be Washburn's wife looking for him or the rest of the family from that tragic evening back in 1938.

There is another Goatman's Bridge located in Burkburnett, Texas, northwest of Denton near Wichita Falls. This bridge spans Gilberts Creek and can be found past the nearby golf course between the town and Sheppard AFB.

This tale relates to a man who is half-human from the waist up and half-goat from the waist down. Similar stories abound here as in Denton like automobile problems but here the sound of children screaming have been reported.

Hutto 78634

Jake's Hill Bridge

Jake's Bridge located along CR 137 outside of Hutto, Texas which is approximately 30 miles northeast of Austin has been the scene of inexplicable paranormal phenomena for years. Nobody knows the real name for this bridge but apparently there was a simple cotton farmer named Jake who lost quite a bit of money during the Great Depression and in 1931 the price of cotton was at an all time low.

According to the legends, Jake just went crazy and killed his entire family. After realizing what he had done, he hung himself from the bridge that later bore his name. Another version says that he pushed a car off the bridge containing the bodies of his parents and shortly afterwards his house caught fire and he burned to death inside.

Today people say that if you come to bridge, put your car in neutral, it will begin to travel by itself, picking up speed. The bridge looks very level and many paranormal teams have been out there conducting investigations using levels and laser levels and have found no discrepancies in elevation.

Reports of two ghostly children seen nearby have been seen by numerous people, perhaps the family that Jake murdered?

San Marcos 78666

Thompson Island Bridge

The Thompson Island Bridge as it's referred to on various websites is actually called the "San Marcos Bridge" and is located at +29.56333, -97.54333 on CR 232 in Gonzales County, Texas between San Marcos and Nixon. It was built in 1915 and spans the San Marcos River. There are actually two bridges that span the San Marcos River but the other actually crosses the sluiceway.

The bridge is thought to be haunted by a ghost of Confederate solider. He apparently died at the bridge while guarding it from the Union Army. He has been seen in his grey and yellow uniform and armed with a rifle. He has been seen since the 1920s.

In 1939, two men repairing a flat tire on their car were startled by a vision of shirtless figure of a very tall man wearing a rebel cap. Alarmed by the weapon, one of the made a dash for a gun in their car but before they could reach it, the figure had already disappeared.

Saratoga 77585

Bragg Road

A Spooklight is seen on a road locally known as Bragg Road and legend has it that Confederate General Braxton Bragg (1817-1876) once lived on this road when the trains still ran. One night a train ran over him, cutting off his head. The light is supposed to be his ghost returning to search for his missing head. Of course, this is the same basic story that is generally heard about any ghost light. In this case, the only truth to it is that Bragg did indeed live there while he was an executive for the railroad; however, he died in Galveston of natural causes. Another story is that of an ill-fated brakeman, Jake Murphy, who was beheaded by the wheels of a passing train.

All those who claim to have seen this light describe it as moving glow, generally red, which changes in intensity from a soft luminosity to a bright, white light. Its movement varies greatly from a slow, slow glide, just barely moving, to racing like the wind, darting back and forth across the road and jumping through the trees. Sometimes it reverses its direction and other times it approaches from one direction, disappears, and reappears approaching from the opposite direction.

It once perched itself on the windshield of a parked car panicking those inside the vehicle. The *Skeptical Inquirer*, Vol. 16, Summer 1992 believed the lights to be an optical illusion caused by the lay of the land and approaching and receding cars going up and down steep hills which cause the light.

The *National Geographic*, October 1974 went to the site to see for themselves what all the fuss was about. Local religious persons call this area Holy Ghost Thicket and some get a mysterious, supernatural feeling upon entering the thicket. The viewing location is said to be approximately five miles north of Highway 105 on Highway 787. Another article was written about the light by *Fate Magazine* in May of 1961. In 1960, Sheriff Whit Whitaker had to post orders, prohibiting firearms in the area. Some of the onlookers were attempting, unsuccessfully, of course to shoot the lights out of the air.

In 1989, Professor Yoshi-Hiko Ohtsuki visited the area and attempted to photograph and videotape the strange lights. Heavy rains prevented them from seeing the lights however their investigation was carried on the Nippon Television Network in April of that year.

Saratoga is about 39 miles west of Beaumont on Highway 787, north of Highway 105 in Hardin County. Bragg Road is an eight-mile-long dirt pathway through a thicket that lies between the Neches and Trinity Rivers.

VERMONT

Stowe 05672

Emily's Bridge

Emily's Covered Bridge is located in Lamoille County, Stowe Hollow, Vermont and was built around 1844 by John W. Smith. It spans the Gold Brook a distance of 48'. The location of the bridge is 1.8 miles south of junction VT108 on VT100, then 1.3 miles left on Gold Brook Road and just left on Covered Bridge Road.

The bridge is supposedly haunted by a female ghost named Emily that will shake cars that are parked or stopped too long on the structure while others claim to have been clawed or scratched by her. She isn't the friendliest of spirits apparently and this has been going on for almost 150 years. People have heard a female voice, seen mysterious ghostly apparitions, and observed strange lights. Photographs taken on the bridge often don't turn out correctly. They may harbor strange fogs, mists or orbs. Some of these however can have natural explanations.

VIRGINIA

Belfast 24280

Route 19 "Belfast Lights"

Mysterious ghost lights have been seen before much of the land in this region became developed and the population increased. At the time these lights were seen the most, the land involved was mostly farm and cattle grazing land. The sighting area is divided by one main road, a two-lane paved highway and Route 19. In Belfast, there is a particular hollow that runs from the base of Clinch Mountain, bottoming out in the valley below. This particular hollow has at least two very old graveyards, one in particular, the final resting place of several children who died in an influenza epidemic at the turn of the century.

Also, lower down in this hollow, is a house that was witness to its own particular horror. There, a man decapitated his father-in-law with an ax during a heated argument. Some distance above the mentioned graveyards, there is the ruins of an old home where another murder took place. This time the crime was carried out by brother against brother after one caught the other with the first one's wife in a compromising situation.

For quite a number of years there has been a ball of light, about the size of a beach ball that could be seen making its way down the hollow to the public road area. There witnesses have sworn that they have been pursued, sometimes at great speed, by this ball of light, only to have it vanish without a trace after about a mile or so.

A couple was making their way along Route 19 and as they approached the above area, one of the riders noticed what appeared to be a floating ball of light coming across the field in their direction. They slowed the car to get a better look at the blue-white ball and the orb made its way closer until it seemed to hover just behind their car.

Becoming spooked, they took off, gaming speed as they went, only to have the light follow at a steady distance behind. They reached speeds of 50 mph. The orb kept pace and even gained ground on the fleeing passengers. After a moment, the orb rose slightly, and passed over the top of their car, to hang suspended over the hood, keeping pace steadily with the moving car. No matter how fast they drove, it kept up, seeming to float stationary above the hood of the car. Then suddenly, the orb vanished; like turning out a light, and there was no trace of its ever being there.

Clifton 20124

Bunnyman Bridge

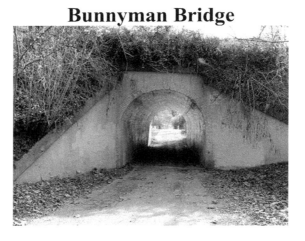

The Bunnyman Bridge is apparently an urban legend that probably started around 1970 stemming from two incidents in Fairfax County, Virginia. One of the variations is of a man dressed up in a bunny costume that goes around killing people with an ax near this underpass. The actual bridge is a concrete tunnel of the Southern Railway overpass on Colchester Road in Clifton.

Two real accounts of a man dressed in a bunny costume swinging an ax in October of 1970 were investigated by Fairfax County Police but both were eventually closed due to lack of evidence. In both cases the Bunnyman was heard to tell their victims that they were trespassing on private property when he became swinging his ax.

Another legend concerns an old insane asylum that was shut down in 1904. During the transfer of prisoners to a new facility the bus crashes killing some inmates, some escaped but eventually all were recaptured except for one. Soon afterwards local residents began to find half-eaten, skinned carcasses of rabbits all around the area. Police identified the missing inmate as Douglas J. Grifon and he became what is today known as the Bunnyman.

Police finally close in on Grifon and nearly apprehend him however he escaped by climbing up the overpass and unfortunately was struck by a train. Officials said they heard unearthly laughter at the exact time the train struck Grifon.

Since that day, people still find carcasses hanging from the trees near the bridge and see a shadowy figure in the tunnel itself. Many folklorists say that this story is completely false as there never was an insane asylum in Fairfax County and court records indicate no person named Grifon ever imprisoned. So this may well be just an urban legend after all but it is still a spooky place at night.

Suffolk 23434

Jackson Road

Two mysterious lights, which sometimes look like one, appear here and when approached, veer off the road and reappear behind the observer. The first sightings of the lights date back over 75 years ago. These lights were reported in an UP dispatch on March 31, 1951 and AP releases in March and April of 1951. Over 300 people showed up one night to view the lights. Deputy Sheriff Beale related that a railroad flagman was killed in about 1912.

To get to the viewing location travel south from Suffolk along Jackson Road and US Hwy 32, near the Great Dismal Swamp in Nansemond County.

(Credit: Mysterious Fires and Lights by Vincent H. Gaddis)

WASHINGTON

Pasco 99301

US Hwy 395

A single moving light which resembles an automobile with a single headlight has been reported here for a number of years. Reports abound of onlookers in cars actually being forced off the road and into ditches by the oncoming light. According to observations, it only appears on foggy, rainy nights.

(Credit: Mysterious Fires and Lights by Vincent H. Gaddis)

Purdy 98335

Purdy Bridge

Purdy Bridge spans Henderson Bay in between Purdy and Purdy Sand Split Park and was built September 29, 1937 at a cost of $62,000. It was designed by Homer M. Hadley and was the first bridge in the United States to utilize a reinforced-concrete box girder design. The bridge was placed on the National Register of Historic Places in 1982. It is located at +47.38382, -122.62851 on Washington 302.

Back in the late 1970s a small child was hit by a car on Purdy Bridge. The guardrails were allegedly put in place since this accident and from time to time you will see a small apparition of him darting across the bridge apparently trying to avoid the car that took his life.

Seattle

Suicide Bridge

What is commonly known by locals in Seattle as Suicide Bridge is actually the George Washington or Aurora Avenue Bridge. The bridge opened up on February 22, 1932 and for what ever reason attracts a lot of jumpers and suicides. It is number two on the list behind the Golden Gate

Bridge in San Francisco with more suicides and deaths. There have been over 230 suicides with fifty of them occurring in the past decade alone. The bridge is 167 feet over the water and an average man will hit the water in less than three seconds at a speed of almost 55 mph.

The bridge was built by Jacobs & Ober however lead engineer Ralph Ober died of a brain hemorrhage in August of 1931 while the bridge was still in construction. It was placed on the National Register of Historic Places on July 16, 1982.

The very first suicide occurred in January 1932 even before the bride was completed. With all of this dark energy present for so many decades, it is any wonder that numerous paranormal events have been witnessed by motorists and pedestrians alike? Other claims include that of a little girl that hung herself from the bridge and her apparition has been reported by some hanging from the bridge.

Allegedly a man and his dog jumped from the bridge and people have reported seeing the chalk marks where this occurred occasionally in addition to the apparitions of a man and a dog by the beach staring at people.

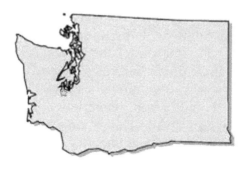

WISCONSIN

Boltonville

Jay Road "Seven Bridges Road"

To get to Jay Road, from I-43 south, take the Highway AA (west) exit to Oostburg, passing through the city. Follow Highway AA as it turns into Highway A and continue west on this road as it bends and turns (13 miles from Oostburg). Take a left on Boltonville Road and follow this road south to the Washington County line, which will take you into the small town of Boltonville. Take a left on Highway X and this road will turn into Jay Road going east. It will end at the shoreline of Lake Michigan, stretching for about twenty five miles past Boltonville.

The reason Jay Road is called Seven Bridges Road is that there are seven distinct bridges along this road. People who visit this area at night often report seeing a strange mist forming in the distance. As one gets closer, the mist forms into what appears to be a woman in a jogging outfit. Apparently a woman was jogging down Jay Road early one morning and was struck by a drunk driver and her body was thrown into a swampy area. Supposedly the body was never recovered. Sometimes motorists pass right through this apparition or it disappears just before you get close enough to pass through it. Other times the jogging woman appears in the automobile and stares at the driver before vanishing!

There is also a stop sign that locals say bleeds. Seen from a distance, it appears as though it is dripping blood but when you get close to it, there is no stop sign at all. This is one of the many tales of the bleeding stop sign which is located in Sheboygan County.

McFarland 53558

Dyreson Road

To reach this location take Highway 51 south of McFarland. Before you reach the Highway B intersection, take a left on Dyreson Road (the road will be marked with a "Wisconsin Rustic Road" sign. The bridge was built back in 1897 and not only the road but the bridge seems to be a center for paranormal activity. The bridge spans the Yahara River in Dane County and was built by the Milwaukee Bridge & Iron Company and can be found at +42.98810, -89.27865 or E. Dyreson Road.

There have been reports of screams and cries which emanate from the area of the old bridge and reports of automobiles seen dangling from the edge of the bridge only to disappear before hitting the water below. People have been chased by a phantom black car while driving on Dyreson Road. The car is described as an older vehicle that seems to keep up no matter how fast you drive and attempts to ram you from behind. The car never actually makes contact with your vehicle but simply vanishes just before it touches the bumper. This story is very similar to the one encountered on Shades of Death Road in New Jersey.

Stevens Point 54481

Red Bridge

Red Bridge was built by Jan Ruta on May 22, 1903 and the town of Hull actually paid him $534.60 for building the bridge; probably a tidy sum of money back then.

A gravel road leads you to Red Bridge and it is said that if you park your car out there at the stroke of midnight and turn off your headlights, the apparition of female will appear on the bridge. Not much more is known about the haunting or who she could be.

Also in Stevens Point on Highway 66 there is another bridge called Bloody Bride Bridge and apparently the legend states that a bride was killed on her wedding night in an auto accident. People have often seen an apparition of woman dressed in a wedding gown walking the area at night. There is a bizarre unsubstantiated report of a police officer seeing this same figure in the middle of the road and unable to stop struck her. He got out to give her first aid and see if she was all right but she wasn't outside but sitting quietly in the back seat of the squad car!

ABOUT THE AUTHOR

Dale Kaczmarek is the President of the Ghost Research Society an international organization of ghost researchers that is based in the Chicago area. He is also author of Windy City Ghosts, Windy City Ghosts II, Field Guide to Spirit Photography and Illuminating the Darkness: The Mystery of Spooklights.

He has also contributed to and appeared in a number of occult-related books including *Dead Zones* by Sharon Jarvis, *The Encyclopedia of Ghosts and Spirits* by Rosemary Ellen Guiley, *More Haunted Houses* by Joan Bingham and Dolores Riccio, *Haunted Places: The National Directory* by Dennis William Hauck, *Sightings* by Susan Michaels, Haunted *Illinois* by Troy Taylor, *Graveyards of Chicago* by Matt Hucke, *Ghosthunting Illinois* by John Kachuba, *A Field Guide to Chicago Hauntings* by Jim Graczyk and many others.

Dale has made a number of television appearances on local and national news programs and has appeared in many documentaries and shows about ghosts and haunted places including *Real Ghosthunters, Sightings, Encounters, The Other Side, Mysteries, Magic and Miracles, Rolanda, Exploring the Unknown,* and *A.M. Chicago* (with Oprah Winfrey) and many others. He has also appeared on dozens of radio and Internet radio programs as well including *Ghostly Talk, Ghost Man & Demon Hunter, Haunted Voices Radio, X-Zone, Para-Nexus* and *Ozark Mountain Radio* among others.

Dale is also a member of the American Association Electronic Voice Phenomena (AA-EVP), International Fortean Organization (INFO), Society for the Investigation of the Unexplained (SITU) and others.

He is also the host of the highly recommended *Excursions Into The Unknown, Inc.,* haunted Chicagoland tours, the only full-time, year-round bus tour in the Chicagoland area. He is CEO and founder of Ghost Research Society Press publishing books on the paranormal and unusual since 2004 and CEO of GRS Productions a production company filming the *Ghosts Across America* DVD series.

He teaches an online course on Ghost Hunting Techniques at IMU, International Metaphysical University (www.intermetu.com) and also tutors and trains up and coming ghost researchers through courses, workshops and seminars that are taught around the country.

His highly successful website www.ghostresearch.org is one of the most active on the Internet today and he receives an average of five paranormal pictures every day. He currently resides with his wife Ruth in Oak Lawn, Illinois.

Coming Soon From
Ghost Research Society Press

FIELD GUIDE TO HAUNTED BED &
BREAKFASTS, INNS & HOTELS
"Where Guests Check-In and Refuse to Check-Out!"
By Jim Graczyk

DEVELOPING A SUCCESSFUL PARANORMAL
RESEARCH TEAM
By Nicole Strickland

FORTY YEARS OF GHOSTHUNTING
"Memoirs of a ghost researcher"
By Dale Kaczmarek

Homepage of the Ghost Research Society Press
http://www.ghostresearch.org/press

Visit Dale Kaczmarek's webpage at:
http://www.ghostresearch.org

Lightning Source UK Ltd.
Milton Keynes UK
UKHW020634170322
400200UK00005B/245